Home-Ec 101

SKILLS FOR EVERYDAY LIVING

HEATHER SOLOS

BETTERWAY HOME
CINCINNATI, OHIO
WWW.BETTERWAYBOOKS.COM

Published by Betterway Home Books, an imprint of F+W Media, Inc., 4700 East Galbraith Road, Cincinnati, Ohio, 45236. (800) 289-0963. First Edition.

 Other fine Betterway Home Books are available from your local bookstore, or online, or direct from the publisher. Visit our website, www.betterwaybooks.com.

15 14 13 12 11   5 4 3 2 1

Distributed in Canada by Fraser Direct
100 Armstrong Avenue, Georgetown, Ontario, Canada L7G 5S4,
Tel: (905) 877-4411

Distributed in the U.K. and Europe by F+W Media International
Brunel House, Newton Abbot, Devon, TQ12 4PU, England, Tel: (+44) 1626 323200,
Fax: (+44) 1626 323319, E-mail: postmaster@davidandcharles.co.uk

Distributed in Australia by Capricorn Link
P.O. Box 704, S. Windsor NSW, 2756 Australia, Tel: (02) 4577-3555

Library of Congress Cataloging in Publication Data
Solos, Heather,
  Home ec 101 : skills for everyday living / by Heather Solos.
    p. cm.
  Includes bibliographical references and index.
  ISBN 978-1-4403-0853-6 (pbk. : alk. paper)
  1. Home economics. I. Title.
  TX145.S695 2011
  640--dc22
                              2010037836

Edited by Jacqueline Musser; Designed by Clare Finney; Production coordinated by Mark Griffin

About the Author

Heather Solos is a former chef, a blogger-turned-author, and a royal pain in the butt. Ten years in the restaurant industry gave Heather the tools she needed to found Home-Ec101.com. Her years in the kitchen inspired her love of food, and the low pay taught her more than she ever wanted to know about living on a budget.

On the Internet, she is charming, witty, and can answer household questions with the greatest of ease. In public, she's a little shy and happiest at the nerd's table riffing on web tech and shiny toys over beer and nachos. At home in the Lowcountry of South Carolina, she's busy with four kids and a patient husband who doesn't seem to mind living in a test kitchen where food must be photographed before it is served. Visit her blog at www.home-ec101.com.

Dedication

This book is dedicated to my family, the Internet, and caffeine; without these, this book would not be possible.

Acknowledgments

I would like to thank the many fine people who work for the National Institute of Food and Agriculture. Their work is a valuable and underutilized resource.

A sincere thank-you to my editor, Jackie, for all the hand-holding.

And, of course, special thanks to my husband, who believed it would all be worth it in the end. I'm still waiting to see if he's right.

Contents

Introduction   6

Section 1: Clean It

1. Getting Started: Tools, Secrets, and the
    Chemistry of Cleaning   10
2. Make It Manageable: Flexible Scheduling   22
3. The Lowdown: Focus on Flooring   32
4. Kitchen Patrol: Win the War Against Grease,
    Grime, and Unintentional Science Projects   42
5. The Great Bathroom Cleansing: Tubs, Toilets,
    and Rubber Gloves   54
6. Dining Rooms and Dusty Dens of Doom:
    Yes, You Do Windows   68
7. Bedroom Antics: Introducing Dust Mites;
    No One Sleeps Alone   80

Section 2: Wash It

8. Stains: Sure You Didn't Spill It   90
9. Odors: Rolling Down the Window Is Not
    Always an Option   100
10. Minor Garment Repair: Beyond Dental Floss
    and Staples   106
11. Laundry: The World's Most Thankless Chore   112

Section 3: Fix It

12. The Bare Minimum Handyman Guide — 124
13. When Good Appliances Go Bad: Avoid Minor Meltdowns — 132
14. Plumbing: Someone Jiggle the Handle Already — 142
15. Throw Rugs and Posters Only Go So Far: Fixing Floors and Walls — 152

Section 4: Cook It

16. Burned Water? There's Hope Yet — 162
17. Outfit Your Kitchen: Cookware and Small Appliances — 170
18. Recipe Rundown: Deciphering Terms and Basic Techniques — 182
19. Pantry Principles: Are You Ready for the Zombie Apocalypse? — 198
20. Meal Planning: Not Just for the Control Freaks — 208
21. Substitutions: I'll Remember to Put It on the List, Promise — 220

Appendix A: Homemade Cleaning Solutions — 232
Appendix B: Dangerous Chemical Combinations — 233
Appendix C: Emergency Preparedness Checklist — 234
Appendix D: Measurements Conversion Charts — 235
Index — 236

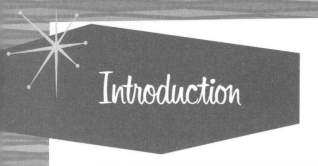

Introduction

I believe life skills are the general population's most underutilized asset.

Cleaning a home?
This goes far beyond extending the life of your carpet or getting the mold out of the shower.

There are psychological aspects in play. Many of us perceive clean as newer, better, even shiny! When I was growing up, my family had a joke that clean cars drove better. It is a familiar phenomenon; as humans there are only so many things we can take in at once, and we rely on general impressions. Walking into a home littered with dirty dishes, laundry, and scattered items does nothing for our general mood or impression of the place—perhaps most significantly when the place is our own home.

Who wouldn't want to go out to escape a pigsty? Going out is fine when it's a choice rather than an avoidance tactic.

Organization—and I'm not talking about the frivolous shopping for fancy boxes kind—helps a person avoid late fees and replacement costs.

Laundry?
Simply keeping an item wearable by removing a stain or by not ruining a delicate item gives a person the ability to keep a little more money in her pocket. Having to buy underwear because nothing is clean is the antithesis of frugality. I'm just sayin'.

Home repair?

There is a satisfaction that goes beyond the money saved when you do it yourself. People like to feel accomplished, which is the reason networks like DIY and HGTV are so successful. Have you ever seen an emergency plumbing bill? How aggravating would it be to learn that the call could have been prevented with a plunger? Basic appliance maintenance and repair can go a long way toward improving the life span and efficiency of larger household investments.

Cooking?

Learning to cook is a process. I strongly believe a series of successes in the kitchen gives a person confidence and the desire to try again.

It doesn't matter how much cooking experience you have. I want to meet you where you are. Some people grow up believing stirring a boxed mix together is cooking. That's fine. My goal isn't to create feelings of guilt or shame. I want to introduce people to the pleasure of preparing real, enjoyable food.

"We don't do great things in life. We do small things with great love."
–Mother Theresa

Using convenience foods because they are convenient is one thing; relying on them daily is expensive long term. Each time someone decides to try his hand at a dish instead of opening a box or ordering out is a win. I get a lot of e-mail from people who are just finding their legs in the kitchen. It absolutely makes my day when someone sends an e-mail to say, "I made my girlfriend dinner and she loved it!"

Nutritionally, I'm trying to broaden palates. It's hard to be healthy over a long period of time with a three-vegetable rotation. But if you're a three-vegetable reader, I'm not judging. Just think of it as a starting point.

It makes good sense to take advantage of seasonal and local produce whenever possible. I see doing so as frugality in the broadest sense of the term: It's making an informed choice to purchase the most beneficial product rather than the one offered at the lowest immediate cost. In addition, supporting a local farmer keeps money in the local economy, including the local tax system, which supports local schools. Long term, that can impact the willingness of other companies to invest in the area; an educated workforce is important.

From keeping your home clean and in good repair to preparing your own food, self-sufficiency rocks. Having an understanding of the domestic arts gives you a sense of control over your life.

Clean It

ONE

Getting Started: Tools, Secrets, and the Chemistry of Cleaning

Dirt happens. If you're browsing along hoping to find a miracle, a simple buy–Brand–X–and–you'll–never–clean–again cure, I hate to break your heart, but you'll be sorely disappointed. Granted, the time and energy cleaning requires can be streamlined and targeted to be as efficient as possible. With the right tools and knowledge, keeping a clean home becomes second nature. Out of habit you'll say, "Excuse the mess," and guests will reply, "What mess?" without lying through their teeth or teetering on the edge of the sofa insisting they are neither hungry nor thirsty.

If there is one question I'm asked more than any other, it has to be, "How can I have a clean home without actually doing anything?" Answer: You hire out.

It's not all the same

Organizing, cleaning, and sanitizing are three different jobs. Organizing is finding a place for things; cleaning is removing dirt and grime; and sanitizing is the process of reducing microbes (that's germs and bacteria) to a safe level.

Let's define our terms, shall we? Organized means a home where everything is put away. A clean home is one where dirt and grime do not reign supreme; a sanitary home is one in which it is safe to cook a meal without the local health inspector having a case of the vapors; a sterile home does not exist. Got it? It's perfectly possible to live in an unorganized, but clean and sanitary home; it just takes a lot more work.

Some homes are quite easy to maintain, and in most cases these dwellings belong to single workaholics who enjoy eating out. If you live alone, pick up after yourself, and are rarely home, then yes, a home takes little effort to clean. A quick wipe down of the kitchen and the bathroom, plus vacuuming, dusting, and occasionally waving a mop in the general area of any hard flooring will keep things tidy.

Once other people (whether of the full-grown or less-so variety) enter the picture, a home just doesn't stay as clean. Humans, by nature, are nasty creatures; always shedding hair or skin; carrying in dust and pollen from outside; and smudging light switches and doorjambs with the oils on their skin. Only the very sheltered—or very lucky—haven't seen what can happen to a neglected bathroom. Maybe in ten years scientists will find the gene responsible for the expression of self-discipline; until then we're stuck with a choice: either hire out or clean up.

Here's a hint, if no one who visits your home is ever hungry or thirsty, it may be time to take a hard, unbiased look at your cleaning habits.

Secret No. 1: An Organized Home is Easier to Clean

Some of you will try to ignore the next bit, but soldier on. As much as it hurts, organization is the magic bullet. I'm sorry, I know you may not want to hear it, but it's true.

Parents with small children—and clean homes—tend to take a basket approach to organization. Why is this? It's due to the Second Law of Thermodynamics, which states a closed system tends toward a state of low energy and high chaos.* If you don't believe me, think of the average dorm room early on a Saturday morning, a perfect illustration of low energy and high chaos. At some point some energy has to be added to the system, and who has the least energy to spare? That's right, people with young kids. The basket approach wrangles small amounts of chaos into inoffensive, semi-contained systems. When junk is corralled and out of sight, it can be as chaotic as it wants.

Artistic types, quit hyperventilating! By no means am I suggesting an investment in coordinating boxes, label makers, and pocket protectors. Use mason jars for your paintbrushes, a tackle box for the beadwork, whatever strikes your fancy. The point is to clear as many horizontal spaces of clutter as possible. If you live alone, your organizational system doesn't have to make sense to others for it to work, but be prepared to continually explain your system when entertaining guests. If others utilize the space, it would be worthwhile to give thought to grouping like with like.

Whether you are a piler or a filer by nature, make sure you have a way to sort paperwork before it is out of control. Try hanging files or letter trays depending on your personality. For transparency's sake, I'm a piler who gets fed up from time to time and files. If you have magazines piling up, donate them to an elementary school, nursing home, or free clinic. Some libraries also accept donations. If there is an article you simply must keep, scan it or take a picture of it with a digital camera.**

The good news is once everything in your home has a place to go, it's very simple to keep a house tidy. Just get into the habit of putting your stuff away. Seriously, just picking up after yourself, putting shoes in the

---

* This is in direct contrast to the fourteenth law of child rearing: Any sugar-addled child will remain in a state of high energy and high chaos.

** Ones and zeros take up a lot less space than paper.

closet, laundry in a hamper, and trash in the proper receptacle will reduce the amount of time and energy needed to clean your house.

Horizontal surfaces attract junk, I don't know why. It's probably something Clausius, Gibbs, and Boltzmann never had to concern themselves with (yes, those are the guys behind that second law we just discussed). Perhaps their mothers or spouses should have given them a chance to observe the phenomenon in the wild—it would be better understood.

Putting your junk away reduces cleaning and sanitizing your home to a matter of removing dirt and germs. It takes thirty seconds to wipe down an empty counter but considerably longer to clear it, wipe it down, wait for it to dry, and then return the items before moving on to the next surface.

Secret No. 2: Each Home Has Its Cleaning Challenges

Why are some houses dirtier than others?

Many factors affect the amount of dirt and grime in a home. These factors go beyond the number of occupants and square footage and include:

- Heating and cooling system—forced air or radiant
- The age of the home—history is messy
- The type of flooring—carpet or hard surface
- The furniture—upholstered or leather
- The composition of the walls—Sheetrock or plaster.

It all plays a part. Dust and pollution enter through open doors and windows. Burning cheap candles can create soot. Frying, whether pan or deep, aerosols grease, allowing it to float and cling to walls or ceilings. In a small home, steam from showers has less room to disperse and clings to the walls. In humid climates, mold and mildew feel more at home. Whatever the reason, everyone has something to complain about.

The occupants of a household also offer different levels of dirt. Individuals under 4 feet (122cm) tall are more likely to smear jelly on the windows, or if it's the young couple smearing jelly, I really just don't want to know. The typical teenager brings a variety of interesting odors into the mix.

Smoking

Speaking of odors, smokers have their own set of cleaning issues. Smoke is sticky and clings to walls and ceilings; if the walls aren't washed on occasion, they will need to be painted more frequently. Additionally, smoking drastically increases the amount of dust and odors in a home. Smoke permeates fabric and upholstered furniture, making it difficult to rid a home of the smell.

Pets

Animals bring a whole new level of dirt into the mix, to say nothing of odors. If it's a cat, there's fur and cat litter to contend with. Dogs track in dirt, leave nose prints, and occasionally find something dead to roll in—hands down one of their most annoying traits. Birds? Even a parakeet can produce an amazing number of feathers and scatter its seed hulls to the four winds.

Size

Those with small living spaces soon find organization becomes a vital and ongoing effort. Those with larger homes have more surface area to clean.

The Chemistry of Cleaning

Choosing the right tool makes cleaning a home easier. Notice I didn't say more interesting; for that I rely on an MP3 player loaded with podcasts and music. Before we get started, it's time to take the Home-Ec 101 safety oath:

> *I solemnly swear to always read the label, test in an*
> *inconspicuous area, not feed the mogwai* after midnight,*
> *and never mix chemicals without research.*

* OK, so the mogwai thing is just a *Gremlins* joke, wherein I reveal my age and inability to progress past random 1980s culture. Interestingly, a mogwai/hedgehog hybrid would make for a bountiful source of scouring pads … Just add water!

Did you know certain combinations of household chemicals, such as chlorine bleach and ammonia, create a reaction that may have deadly consequences? (And here you thought chemistry was boring.) Sounds easy enough to avoid, right? The problem is bleach and ammonia show up in unexpected places. See Appendix B for a more complete list of household chemical combinations to avoid. Always read the labels of cleaning products, and reread them if they've been reformulated. Usually you can tell by labels screaming *new* or *improved*.** Lastly, never store chemicals in unmarked containers. Appendix A has several recipes for mixing up your own household cleaning products. Clearly label these containers and always note if bleach or ammonia is present in the solution.

If you visit any big-box store, you may observe that cleaning products usually fill several aisles with a dizzying array of choice. Does anyone really need 172 products to clean a home? Nope, but then again, I didn't major in marketing.

Are some of these products more effective than others? Possibly, but a lot of it comes down to personal preference and that preference is based on habit, nostalgia, the scent, or even on marketing. When choosing a cleaning product, ask yourself:

- Does this product save enough time to justify the extra expense? This is actual man hours on the clock, not time that would otherwise be spent vegging out on the sofa.
- Is this product worth the environmental cost? Some disposable products may save time, but many are not recyclable and there is also an environmental cost in their production.
- Do I really need a different product for this task? Many products can be used in multiple areas of the home. A laminate counter is a laminate counter whether it is found in the kitchen or the bathroom. Porcelain is porcelain in the kitchen and the bathroom; the same goes for linoleum and hardwood.

** This just means they still haven't gotten it right.

- Is this product really better for the environment? There is no need to go out and purchase organic bamboo or cotton cleaning rags if you already have old T-shirts or towels at home.*
- Is this product really safer because it's natural? Food for thought: Nightshade, strychnine, and hemlock are all perfectly natural.

Types of Cleaning Products

Did you know that any chemical used for cleaning can be called a detergent? This means that the term even applies to plain water. So if every cleaning product is a detergent, how does a consumer decide which cleaning products are right for which job? It helps to learn a little household chemistry. The next section is a brief rundown on the chemistry of some common household cleaning chemicals to help you make an informed decision when purchasing cleaners.

Chemistry Flashback

Pure water has a neutral pH of seven. Lemon juice is an acid with a low pH of two to three, while chlorine bleach, a common base, has a high pH of twelve. Solutions that contain acids are called acidic. Solutions that contain bases are called alkaline.

Soap. Soap is nothing more than fat that has been treated with a strong base. That fat may come from either animals or plants, so if you're vegetarian you may want to put some extra time into your label reading. Remember sodium tallowate is beef tallow (fat) treated with lye. Once fat, vegetable or animal, has been treated with a strong base (or *saponified,* as the chemists say), it develops some interesting properties. Part of the soap molecule is attracted to water and part of the same molecule is repelled by it. This allows the soap molecules to surround dirt and oils and suspend them in water or

---

* The three Rs of environmentalism are: *Reduce, Reuse, Recycle,* not Run-Out-and-Buy-New-Crap.

solution. The hardness of your water can significantly reduce the effectiveness of your soap. If lots of soap molecules are wasted by surrounding dissolved minerals in the water, there won't be as many available to clean the dirt off of a surface. Soaps vary from one to the next in their harshness, which is important to know because sometimes you actually want to leave some oils behind, on your hands and face for example. You can also find soaps that contain different amounts (or lack there of) of perfumes and dyes.

Solvent: A substance, usually a liquid, that can dissolve or disperse another substance.

This brings us to our next fancy word, *surfactants*. You've heard the axiom oil and water don't mix? Surfactants help reduce the surface tension of liquids, which actually makes it possible for the two to mix. When oil and water can occupy the same space, it is easier to remove grease from surfaces because the oils can come into solution—that's the watery part—and be wiped away. All soaps are, by nature, surfactants, but they aren't the only type that exists.

Degreasers, window cleaners, and multisurface cleaners. Degreasers are typically an alkaline solution containing surfactants. These are particularly useful for—wait for it—removing grease. You may recognize Pine-Sol, Formula 409, and Simple Green as examples.

Glass cleaners also tend to be mildly alkaline solutions containing ammonia, a surfactant; a solvent such as isopropyl (rubbing) alcohol; and perfume to mask the scents of the other chemicals. Glass cleaners and degreasers share a lot of the same territory, which explains multisurface cleaners.**

Dusting. Dusting sprays and furniture polish are not interchangeable products, though they are sold in the same section of the cleaning aisle. Dusting sprays are used to wipe away dust; some dusting sprays contain

---

** Water is perhaps the greatest multisurface cleaner ever invented, but no one will let me patent it.

electrostatically charged ingredients in an attempt to repel future dust. Furniture polish is used to restore moisture and prevent damage to the finish of wood furniture.

Scouring powders. Scouring powders are powders that sand or scour away stains. Care must be taken when using these products, as some brands have more abrasive formulas than others and can damage some surfaces.*

Always read the label carefully and follow the manufacturer's instructions. Never use scouring powders on nonstick cookware. These products may be acidic or alkaline depending on their composition. Common brand names include Comet and Bar Keepers Friend. Always rinse a surface thoroughly after using a scouring powder to prevent a reaction with the next cleaning product.

Floor cleaner. Floor cleaners typically contain a combination of household chemicals specific to the type of floor for which they are designed, although most contain a degreaser or soap and surfactants. We'll delve further into these in chapter 3.

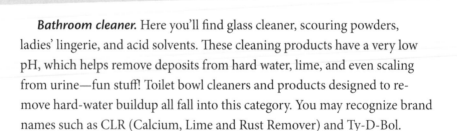

Food-Grade Products

If you want to use scouring powder on standard cookware, be sure to use a food-grade product—safe to use on utensils and food preparation surfaces.

Bathroom cleaner. Here you'll find glass cleaner, scouring powders, ladies' lingerie, and acid solvents. These cleaning products have a very low pH, which helps remove deposits from hard water, lime, and even scaling from urine—fun stuff! Toilet bowl cleaners and products designed to remove hard-water buildup all fall into this category. You may recognize brand names such as CLR (Calcium, Lime and Rust Remover) and Ty-D-Bol.

* Caution: Be wary of any gel or paste product that lists pumice as an ingredient—it's essentially a liquid cheese grater.

Disinfectants. We're entering controversial territory: It's time to talk disinfecting and sanitizing.** It's controversial as "some"*** believe our hyperclean environments may be part of our population's growing problem with asthma and allergies. There are also myriad websites giving misleading advice about the disinfecting properties of white vinegar. Any chemical that can reduce the number of microorganisms on a surface can be legally described as a disinfecting agent. In many cases, white vinegar is adequate, but if someone in the home has a compromised immune system, you must choose an approved sanitizing agent and it must be used in a manner consistent with the manufacturer's guidelines. Applied improperly, some of the effectiveness of sanitizing agents could be compromised, and some biocides, such as tea tree oil applications at too low of a dilution, can actually drive antibiotic resistance in some bacteria. Remember, only a few chemicals meet the standards of a sanitizing agent, and even then, they must be at certain dilutions. The most commonly recommended sanitizer is chlorine bleach. Do not confuse sanitary with sterile. Sanitary implies the number of microorganisms have been reduced to within acceptable and safe limits. Sterile is used to describe methods that kill all microorganisms, such as for medical procedures.

Wake up, chem class is over.

Cleaning Equipment

Now that you have an idea of what goes into the cleaning products that are out there, let's take a peek at the equipment you'll want in your cleaning arsenal:

- A broom and dustpan
- Vacuum, preferably with attachments. If you have allergies, invest in a vacuum with a HEPA filter to help control the amount of dust (and dust mites)

** The janitorial Roe v. Wade.
*** Note "some" also believe in tinfoil hats, magnetic bracelets, and "The Force."

- Mop: string or sponge. Some people prefer to have two mops, one for the kitchen and one for the bathroom(s)
- Bucket (two is helpful)
- A scrub brush. I prefer one with a pointed end to reach into corners. If you have tile, consider a grout brush.
- Toilet scrub brush and optional container for storage. If possible, have one for each bathroom.
- Rags. These will accomplish almost any job a paper towel can. If a washer or dryer is available, experiment with using rags as often as possible. Just be sure to rinse and wring out before placing them in the dirty laundry pile (unless you list mildew removal under your list of "likes").
- Spray bottles (optional). These are inexpensive and very useful for applying homemade cleaners.
- Rubber gloves*
- Squeegee

Now that we have a good idea of what it takes to clean a home, I have good news and bad news. You can own all the top-of-the-line products and tools and still have a filthy home. Why? It takes effort to undo the dirt, and that dirt never stops accumulating. The good news is, put into practice, a fairly simple routine can keep a home clean and sanitary.

Dirt builds over time, but you don't have to see a difference to keep it at bay. Sure, it's not as satisfying to wipe something that already looks clean, but I promise it takes a lot less effort. Take the lowly toilet. This household feature is constantly collecting dirt, hair**—look, I don't get it either, I just clean it up—and germs. If each morning the bowl received a fifteen second scrub (with or without a cleaning agent) and the seat, rim, and that obnoxious area between the seat and the tank received a quick wipe down with a rag or disposable wipe, the random hairs and spatter never really have a

---

* Hazmat suits are generally overkill for most home use.
** Home-Ec 101 Pro Tip: If your toilet is sporting a goatee or perm, it's time to increase scheduled cleanings; it's also time for a special chat with other household members.

chance to accumulate. Whether you like the idea or not, there comes a time when most of us end up sharing some face time with the porcelain bowl. I try to ensure the ordeal is as pleasant as possible.

Everyone has cleaning issues specific to their own living situations. The next several chapters cover a deep room-by-room clean. Organizing is very different than cleaning, and unless there is a huge press for time, it's best to organize first, then clean. With a notable exception, always clean areas used for food preparation.*** Once a room has received a deep clean, it's possible to enter into a maintenance routine such as the one outlined in chapter 2.

Don't be alarmed if your first deep clean takes a long time. This is normal and happens to everyone, except liars and your one-upping cousin Martha. Sometimes we get knocked for a loop by a career change, the birth of a baby, the death of a family member, or even something less dramatic like a vacation. It can be months or weeks later, when there is a moment to breathe, that the realization that it's time for a deep clean sets in.

*** If not, say hello to "Mr. Dysentery," but don't worry, he's just passing through.

TWO

Make It Manageable: Flexible Scheduling

There are many reasons to make keeping house a priority, and emulating Donna Reed isn't one of them. As children, the punishments for not performing household chores are pretty obvious: Don't do the dishes, no television. Straightforward, simple, and fairly effective. As adults, provided we've managed to cut the apron strings, the consequences of laziness aren't always as clear. Housework seems like one of those areas that it's safe to let go. It's easy to avoid company, and aside from that, who really cares if the sheets are rarely washed? No one can see the dust if the blinds aren't open, and who needs to cook when there's pizza to order?

There's a lot to be said for self-expression, but living in a pit only expresses a lack of self-respect and motivation.

Living in a clean home does wonders for emotional well-being. Having control over one's surroundings adds a feeling of empowerment even in troubled times. Even high-end furnishings appear trashy if a room is in disarray. A set of Le Creuset dishware looks just like any other dirty dishes in a full sink. If the psychological reasons for getting off your butt aren't enough motivation, what about the financial reasons? Housework is all about saving time and money. If you can find your clothes, keys, and briefcase/purse/backpack, there's a lot less time involved in leaving the house than old Joe Schlub has to spend.* Managing to show up for work on time is a significant milestone on the maturity timeline.

Are you environmentally conscious? The environment is another huge reason to clean, and as long as the products you choose aren't horrendously toxic,** making do with the items already in your household is the most important *R* of the *Reduce, Reuse, Recycle* axiom. As an example, regularly vacuuming can extend the life of flooring by years. Maintaining appliances means purchasing fewer replacements, and frequently it also means lower utility bills.

Protect Your Investments

Regular cleaning protects the money that has already been spent. This is especially true if furnishings were financed; without maintenance they depreciate even faster.

Again with the "But I'm artistic!" argument. Really? Here's the thing: roaches don't discern the subtle difference between laziness-induced filth and that caused by eschewing the cultural norm. Art is not an excuse for being a slob. Fight the man, make your own cleaning products, weave your own clothes, buy handmade, recycle, up-cycle, stay up all night, sleep all day, dance, paint, sing, whatever. Just wash the dishes, sweep the floor, and take out the trash, *you damn dirty apes!* Sorry, channeled my inner Charlton Heston for a moment there.

* Sorry Joe, had to call you out.
** Even Melvin the Mop Boy from *The Toxic Avenger* prefers nontoxic alternatives.

A chore schedule doesn't have to be oppressive to be effective. Decent hygiene has a few daily demands:*

- Clean up after meals. This includes properly storing leftovers, wiping food preparation areas, and doing the dishes.
- Wipe the sink and toilet with either a disposable wipe or a rag the last time the room is used for the day.
- Use a squeegee or rag to wipe down the shower or tub before getting out.
- Place the laundry in the hamper.
- Clean up spills as they happen.
- Large households should also sweep or vacuum high-traffic areas. This chore should be shared by all household members.

Page 25 has a quick reference weekly chore chart. That's no so bad, is it?

Daily Chores Explained

Mondays

Strip the beds and replace the sheets. Do laundry as necessary and clean up the laundry station, whether this is a room or merely a nook where laundry is stored until the trip to the laundromat. Put away any clean clothing that has been left out, and place ill-fitting clothing in a bin for donation.

Monday is not necessarily a marathon laundry day, unless this is the method that works for your lifestyle. Households with several people may find it easier to do several loads during the week. Mondays are for catching the items that tend to be put off until later. While in the laundry area, check on the supply level and make sure nothing needs to be added to the shopping list.

Spend just a few minutes wiping down the kitchen, catch the fingerprints on the appliances, sticky spots on the counter, and make sure the kitchen sink doesn't resemble a petri dish.

---

* I make the bed every morning simply to feel accomplished. At least something on the list was crossed off.

Weekly Chore Chart

Day	Big Chore	Fast Chore
Monday	Laundry and Bedding	Kitchen Wipe Down
Tuesday	Floors: Sweep, Mop, Vacuum	15-Minute Pickup
Wednesday	Errands	Car and Entry Cleanup
Thursday	Bathroom(s)	That's enough for one day
Friday	Kitchen Cleanup	15 Minutes Dusting
Saturday	Project Day	
Sunday	Weekly Preparation	

Tuesdays

Time to tackle the floors, hurray! But before dragging out the vacuum, set a timer and spend fifteen minutes putting away items. Focus low, preparing the rooms for an allied assault via vacuum and broom. As time permits, get rid of junk mail, file paperwork, and sort newspapers and magazines for recycling. If you have children, make them help put away their own toys and shoes. Put on their music if that serves as motivation, or try to make a game of the activity. Clearing away the clutter will make quick work of cleaning the floors.

Give each carpeted room a good once-over with the vacuum, paying extra attention to higher traffic areas. Each week, spend a little extra time on one room, using the crevice tool to reach the no-man's-land between the baseboard and the edge of the carpeting. The focus room's flooring should get a good once-over; check the carpeting for stains and treat as necessary. Pull the cushions off the couches and upholstered chairs, and get rid of the

Sharing Household Duties

Dear Home-Ec 101,

My husband and I both grew up in homes where the father worked and the mother largely stayed home and attended to all of the household duties. We both work and sometimes have a hard time agreeing on who should be doing which chores how often, and how well. I tend to feel like I'm expected to do more than my fair share. How can we successfully negotiate housework? I'm really tired of hearing complaints about how I didn't magically know to wash a specific pair of jeans that weren't in the hamper. Ultimately, I would like for everybody to have clear expectations and get things done without it being a constant struggle and source of contention.

Signed,
Bickering in Brentwood

It sounds as though there may be a breakdown in communication. One of you is bound to have a lower tolerance for mess and that person will end up with the lion's share of chores unless boundaries are set. I know it does not sound fun, but you may have to sit down and actually discuss the division of chores. Consider making a list of chores in three columns: daily, weekly, and seasonal. Then, taking turns, take colored pencils or markers and indicate the chores you don't mind with one color and chores you abhor with another. This should help fairly divide the list. For the chores you both hate, institute a rotation, but the rotation should last long enough that it would be obvious if one of you were slacking. Passive aggression should not be tolerated; it will only increase resentment. Letting him know what you need is not nagging; additionally, expecting him to intuit those needs is unrealistic. Extend him the courtesy of telling him your expectations and ask him to do the same for you. Best of luck.

crumbs, but pocket the change. Throw rugs should be shaken outside and washed if necessary. Sweep or vacuum the solid-surface flooring, and mop or dust mop these areas, too.

Wednesdays

Welcome to errand days. It's a day to plan appointments, carry them out, or make the phone calls that are so easy to avoid. Drop off donations or pick up the dry cleaning. Setting aside one day a week for these obnoxious chores makes them easier to remember. If Wednesdays don't work for your schedule, simply swap them with a day that does. The point isn't for every family to grocery shop on Wednesday, rather it's to have a time for it to happen so purchases can be planned and budgeted. Wednesdays are also a good day to schedule service calls as the post-weekend rush is over and there is a higher chance your service person won't just be going through the motions, trying to make five o'clock Friday. Over time, household members realize that if they have a request, it needs to be made before the trip to the store occurs. Sometimes this takes firmness and repetition, but it sinks in … eventually.

Every Effort Counts

As soon as children are able to operate the vacuum, let them help with this chore. However haphazard the lines are, don't go back over their work to realign them. Even poor vacuuming helps remove some dirt from carpeting. Praise the child; just make sure he isn't the only one assigned a high traffic area. Older children can be coached in proper technique.

Thursdays

Daily wipe downs are the key to keeping Thursdays from getting out of control. Small households can usually get away with focusing on one bathroom per week, unless small children are present. If there are several bathrooms and multiple members in the household, divide and conquer; just make sure the delegates understand the chore. There's a difference between nagging and outlining baseline expectations.

Friday

KP duty falls on Friday. Start with a quick round of dish patrol: Check every room and gather any stray utensils or glasses. If there are pots or pans that have been neglected—I mean soaking—scrub them. Scrape the spills from the stove and wipe down the appliances. Give cabinets and countertops a good wipe down, the kind where small appliances are actually moved, wiped under, and replaced. Clear the refrigerator of any unintentional science projects, wiping the shelves as you go.

After the kitchen has been reassembled, spend fifteen minutes dusting and doing fingerprint patrol. Carry a damp rag for smudges on switch plates and doorjambs. Use the vacuum's soft bristle brush to vacuum as much as possible and use the damp rag to get the rest. Rotate where the dusting begins to avoid neglecting any rooms. Start one week in the living room and another in a bedroom. If your household has a lot of knick-knacks and tchotchkes that require dusting, it may be necessary to increase the amount of time spent on this chore.

Value Your Time

Don't underestimate the value of your time. Naturally there will be exceptions and emergencies, but don't be a pushover willing to drop everything for anyone at any given time. A good rule of thumb: If you wouldn't dream of interrupting your best friend, spouse, or parents with the request, expect the same courtesy.

Saturday

Project day covers everything from yard maintenance to room painting. By no means should every Saturday be devoted only to housework; even homeowners should have social lives.*

Sunday

Today's big chore is preparing for the week ahead. Find all the library books or movies that need to be returned. Pack book bags or briefcases, menu plan, and find missing keys or shoes. Look at the calendar and get a sense of what's coming. Are there days that will be too busy for meal preparation? Plan foods to grab and go. Are there meetings or events that require nice clothing or a haircut? Having a plan prevents panic the night before—or worse, the morning of—important events.

Monthly Tasks

Some chores need only be performed monthly. Work them in as their room comes up in the rotation or slip them in on Saturdays.

- Dust: walls, light fixtures, fans, vents, and blinds. While dusting the vents, inspect the filter for the HVAC unit. It should be replaced at least every ninety days or when it becomes clogged. Most walls can be dusted with a lamb's-wool-style duster or feather duster. Walls

---

* Maybe not this homeowner, but you've been reading the footnotes all along, haven't you?

painted with semigloss or satin washable paints can be dusted with a slightly damp rag. To keep this chore from becoming overwhelming, focus on a single room a week.

- The great cobweb walk-through. Charlotte has got to go, so fasten a pillowcase over the business end of the broom and search high and low for cobwebs.
- Inspect and test smoke alarms.
- Wash blankets.

Seasonal Chores

Some chores are seasonal. Work these in as applicable.

Spring

- ☐ Wash windows, indoors and out.
- ☐ Inspect screens for damage to prevent inviting bugs inside along with the fresh air.
- ☐ Clean and inspect gutters.
- ☐ Clean patio furniture in anticipation of nice weather and outdoor events.
- ☐ Have the HVAC unit inspected by a professional to prevent emergency repairs when the hot weather hits.
- ☐ Store blankets and warm clothing.

Summer

- ☐ Inspect the roof for damage. There are typically more workers available during the summer months.
- ☐ Inspect decks and patios; repair if necessary.
- ☐ Clean the clothes dryer vent and exhaust hose.
- ☐ Inspect caulk around showers and tubs and replace if necessary.
- ☐ Check under all sinks, behind toilets, tubs, showers, and the water heater for leaks.

☐ Check the hoses on the clothes washer, dishwasher, and ice maker. Look for cracks or bubbles and replace as necessary.

Fall

☐ Replace the batteries in smoke alarms.
☐ Clean and put away patio and outdoor furniture.
☐ Drain and store hoses.
☐ Have the furnace, boiler, or chimney and flue inspected.
☐ Wash exterior windows.
☐ Inspect seals around doors and windows, and repair if necessary to prevent drafts during cold weather.
☐ Check gutters and downspouts.
☐ Drain sediment from hot water heaters.
☐ Take blankets and warm clothing out of storage.

Winter

☐ If you live in an area that gets snow, place waterproof mats near each entryway.
☐ Clean out the pantry.
☐ Spend time on organizational projects while the weather is bad.

THREE

The Lowdown: Focus on Flooring

Some of the most destructive dirt in a home hitches a ride in on footwear. It takes an average of six steps to shed the freeloading grit from your shoes. If a home doesn't have a good doormat or a runner to catch the offending filth, the flooring bears the brunt of the damage. It's not actually the dirt that wreaks havoc, it's our pesky tendency to walk on our flooring.* Our footsteps grind the tracked-in grit into the floor surface, which can cause tiny nicks and scratches on hard flooring and break down fibers in carpeting.

Sometimes, after a long day, I dream of a home with rubber-coated walls, painted cement floors with a convenient drain in the corner, and a fire sprinkler system straight off a Navy battleship. I could send the kids to bed and clean the house with just the pull of a handle. For better or for worse, we've not yet had any input on the design of a home. I'm also willing to bet this dream will fade as the children grow. Someday I'll be able to look at flooring without doing a mental inventory of how well it masks the presence of dirt. Industrial chic isn't my thing anyway. I'm far too upbeat to pull off an affected, jaded pretense.

* We're still waiting on our hover boards, Dr. Brown.

Whether your home has wall-to-wall builder's grade carpet or inlaid polished marble, removing dirt is the key to the longevity of your investment. Each entryway should have a doormat or throw rug to catch tracked-in dirt. Doormats and runners should be taken outside and shaken frequently. Both high-traffic zones and pet living areas should be swept or vacuumed daily. Consider adding throw rugs in front of favorite chairs and placing runners in busy hallways. These cheap additions can significantly extend the life of carpeting by protecting the fibers from excessive wear, which causes crush damage and matting.

Areas with moderate traffic, such as bedrooms and bathrooms, can be swept or vacuumed once a week. In some areas of the United States, many homes have a mudroom, which is a place to kick off filthy shoes before entering the living area. The downside is it's yet another place to sweep.

Tools and Techniques for Hard Floors

Brooms

Brooms designed for indoor use come in two main styles, soft, plastic bristle or straw.** Newer, smooth, undamaged flooring is best cleaned with a soft-bristled broom; straw brooms are coarser and are a better choice for rough, worn flooring. There is a chance straw brooms could damage more delicate finishes. Brooms with angled heads are useful for sweeping under cabinets.

Before sweeping a room, turn off any fans and clear the room of all non-essential personnel.*** Simply sweeping stirs up dust and there is no need for it to be blown further than it needs to be.

The actual sweeping motion is fairly simple. Stand with your feet about shoulder width apart, and with your dominant hand, grasp the handle near

---

** Your mother-in-law may mention a third, but as a rule, that one is for transportation only. Stirrups interfere with the proper sweeping technique.

*** An animal's or child's attraction to dirt is never more evident than when crumbs and dust are concentrated in one small pile. Children have been known to appear from blocks away to poke at paper shreds and dust bunnies. A closed door is only a temporary solution, and be prepared for much wailing and gnashing of teeth as the union is denied.

the top. Your other hand should be holding the handle somewhat near your waist. The bristles should make full contact with the floor, but not bend. Pressing too firmly may scratch the floor with grit and weaken the straw. Too little pressure and the dirt will be left behind. Use short strokes and work the dirt into a pile, being careful not to backtrack over the swept portion until the room has been swept. Sweep the debris into a dustpan and dispose. Allow children and pets to return to the room only if you'd like to repeat the cleaning process in the near future.

Sweeping

There are two basic methods to sweeping a room.

- The perimeter method works best in square rooms. Simply pick one corner and sweep inward along the walls. Work around the room, spiraling inward, until the dirt pile reaches the center of the room.
- Hallways and long, rectangular rooms are best swept with an end-to-end method. Start at one wall and work toward the other, pulling the pile along with you until the far wall is reached.

Dust Mops

Dust mops are useful in homes with lots of tile or hardwood, but they should be used only after the flooring has been cleared of sand and grit. If a dust mop catches sand in its fibers, it quickly transforms into a wide-path manual-powered sanding belt. Typically dust mops are microfiber or cotton. Dust mop treatment is available, but plain water works just fine. Before placing the removable pad onto the head of the dust mop, wet it with warm water and wring it well. Water helps dust cling to the material. Use an S-type pattern when dust mopping. Start at one end of the room, close to the baseboards, and walk to the other end of the floor. Turn the mophead and overlap the path by several inches, then repeat the process until out of patience or flooring. Rinse out the mophead, wring it well, and either hang it to dry or add it to the laundry pile.

Mops

There are two basic kinds of mops, string or sponge. The best mop for a job depends on the type of flooring and personal preference. Most homes have smooth flooring such as laminate or tile, but there are homes with painted cement, textured tile, or brick flooring, and the rough surface of these floorings can shred a sponge mop to bits. Smooth floors are best cleaned with a sponge mop, but a string-style mop can be used. If you have a string mop, be sure you either have a wringer on your bucket or the mop is equipped with one. Too much water is never a good thing.

The same rules for dust mopping apply to damp mopping. Be sure the floor is free of sand and grit before beginning. Fill a bucket with your cleaning solution, dip the mop into the cleaning solution, wring out all the excess water, begin mopping.

Begin in the corner furthest from your escape route and mentally map out a series of 4' × 4' (122cm × 122cm) squares. Mop the floor using short strokes; when damp mopping hardwood, always go in the direction of the wood grain to prevent streaking. Each time a section of the floor is completed, either rinse the mop or swish it thoroughly in the cleaning solution. Rewring it and continue until the floor has been completely mopped. Some cleaning solutions need to be rinsed from the floor. In these cases, repeat the process with warm water in place of the cleaning solution. Once the room has been mopped, try not to flip out when someone knocks over the OJ, because it will happen.

Just as a lot of attention needs to be paid to chemicals when cleaning a bathroom, the same is true for mopping a floor. Hardwood floors should be

Bleach Is Bad News

Never use bleach on linoleum or hardwood flooring. The high pH can damage the finish.

cleaned with a pH-neutral cleaner as recommended by the manufacturer. Many modern hardwood floors have a warranty on their finish, and cleaning with a product other than one suggested by the manufacturer may void the warranty.

Types of Flooring

Linoleum. Linoleum and vinyl flooring are not interchangeable terms. Linoleum is manufactured from linseed oil, pine rosin, or ground cork and should be treated with the same care as hardwood. PH-neutral cleaners are best, as both acids and bases can cause microscopic pitting, which, just like physical scratching caused by grit, dulls the surface and gives dirt plenty of places to hide. If you do not have the manufacturer's recommendation and the flooring is not under warranty, mop with plain dish detergent (about 1 tablespoon per quart of water). Be sure to rinse the flooring well with clean water.

Vinyl. Vinyl flooring should be cleaned with dilute ammonia or dish detergent, unless a specific cleaner has been recommended by the manufacturer. Dilute 1 tablespoon of ammonia per quart of warm water. Rinsing is important to avoid leaving behind a film that will cause the flooring to appear dull.

Ceramic Tile. Sealed ceramic tile flooring is cared for similarly to vinyl flooring. Use the manufacturer's recommended detergent or very diluted

Avoid Abrasives and Oil

Never use abrasive cleaners or steel wool to clean flooring, even if it removes the spill, because it scratches the surface, making it more difficult to clean in the future. Oil-based cleaners are almost always a bad idea when it comes to flooring. Do not use these unless specifically directed by the manufacturer. Never use furniture polish on hardwood; the shine is never worth the increased risk of slips and falls.

dish detergent and follow with a rinse. Acidic cleaners may damage unsealed grout. Grout, the material between the tiles, should be sealed as recommended. The seal protects the grout from stains and damage.

Vacuuming Hard Floors

When it comes to floor care, a good vacuum can be your best bet, even in homes with lots of hard flooring. Just be sure to turn off the beater bar before rolling the vacuum off of the carpet. (Consult the manual for instructions on how to deactivate the beater bar.) If the beater bar spins while the vacuum runs over hard flooring, not only will it scatter debris faster than even the strongest motor can suck, it has the potential to grind in grit, essentially sanding the surface. If your vacuum has hard plastic wheels, they should be checked regularly for embedded grit or debris that could scratch the flooring. Some models have a hard flooring attachment. Typically these have bristles to help catch and pick up dirt. The downside to vacuuming hard flooring is that the dust frequently gets left behind, but a quick once-over with a dust mop once a week keeps dust under control.

Tools and Techniques for Carpeting

Carpet manufacturers have an entire dictionary of terms to describe their wares—bulk, pile, hand, crushing, matting—it can be a little confusing. When vacuuming, the only important thing to know is when to use the

Types of Carpets

Most carpeting is made from four types of fibers:

- **Nylon:** Very durable, withstands wear, resists crushing, and recently its ability to resist stains has been improved through the miracle of science.
- **Olefin:** Frequently used for berber-style carpets and commercial loops. It's quite stain resistant but is prone to matting and damage from crushing. This synthetic material has a very low melting point and loves oil, making greasy stains more difficult to remove.
- **Polyester:** Is the more environmentally friendly synthetic option, but it isn't quite as resilient as nylon. Over time it will mat or show crush damage. Proper maintenance (that is, actually vacuuming) can significantly increase the life span of this lower-cost and fairly stain-resistant option.
- **Wool:** Has a significantly higher initial cost but has a higher resistance to crush damage and is more resilient than synthetic fibers. It is naturally stain resistant.

rotator brush or beater bar and when to turn it off. Residential carpeting has a few basic styles:

Cut pile (which comes in several lengths): Textured pile, Saxony, Frieze, and Plush. Frieze* is the longest of these and is frequently mistaken for shag carpeting. Avoid using a beater bar on Frieze, unless this conflicts with the manufacturer's advice.**

Loop Pile: The carpet fibers are looped. Berber carpeting is an excellent example. Watch out for snags in high traffic areas.

Cut-and-Loop Pile: This (unsurprisingly) is a combination of cut pile and loop pile.

---

* This can only be enunciated with a lip-curling sneer and an atrociously bad French accent, frrr-eee-ieze.

** As a general rule, never beat anything when a simple verbal tirade will do.

Removing Diarrhea from Carpet

Dear Home-Ec 101,

What is the best way to clean diarrhea off of carpet? I'll spare you the exact details, but let's just say it's pretty heinous.

Signed,
Poopy in Peewauket

Oh, dear. Clearly, your day has been crappier than mine.

An immediate, but temporary measure is to use paper towels to blot up as much of the mess as possible, then put some Spray 'n Wash (remember to test in an inconspicuous area first) down on the area and blot. This will help keep the stain from setting. But to clean up the mess entirely, you are going to have to pull out the big guns.

You need some strong suction to be able to remove the mess. Regular household carpet cleaners may not be strong enough for the job. I would rent a commercial machine like a Rug Doctor or call in a professional.

If you choose the DIY route, find an enzymatic cleaner such as Kids 'N' Pets. This cleaner may be found in the pet care aisle or near the carpet cleaners (in many large stores, they carry it in both sections). Place the enzymatic cleaner on the spot and then go over it with the commercial machine. After you have cleaned the mess with the chemical and gotten the stain up, fill the machine with clear water and go over the area again several times. The clear water will not only ensure the carpeting is clean, but it will help rinse out the machine. After all, you don't want to be the customer who returns the machine filled with excrement. That reputation would be hard to shake.

Good luck!

Vacuuming Carpet

Vacuuming carpet sounds simple enough, but there are a few tricks to the trade. Plug in the vacuum and adjust the height to the appropriate level for your type of carpeting. Unless you're vacuuming a Frieze or shag carpeting, the height of the vacuum should allow the beater bar to agitate the carpet a few inches from the head of the unit, but it shouldn't be difficult to push. Begin vacuuming in one corner of the room and vacuum in short strokes that overlap. Work your way in sections until the entire room has been vacuumed, with each area of carpeting receiving several passes from the appliance. High-traffic areas should be vacuumed across and against the flow of traffic to help reduce crushing and matting. If your vacuum seems to be losing its suction, check out chapter 13 for some basic troubleshooting on appliances.

Vacuum Regularly

Vacuum deeply, a minimum of once a week, regardless of the size of the household. For each person or pet in the household, add an additional quick vacuum for high-traffic areas.

Steam Cleaning

Carpeting also needs to be cleaned with hot water extraction, better known as steam cleaning, periodically. Refer to your warranty before using a rented machine. Some warranties are extremely picky about the cleaning methods.

Spot-Treating and Stains

Between steam cleanings, spot treatment for stains is occasionally necessary. It's useful to have a stack of white towels or rags on hand. (These are the most absorbent and don't bleed colors. Find them in the automotive aisle.) Whenever tackling stains or spills, first remove any solid particles by hand (or plastic bag or glove) and then blot, never rub, any remaining liquid. There is an exception for mud—let it dry before cleaning. Once it has solidified, break up the clump and vacuum thoroughly before addressing any staining. One of the biggest problems with many commercial stain

Test First, Treat Second

Always test your carpeting in an inconspicuous area before attempting spot removal!

removers is they offer only a temporary solution and may leave the area more vulnerable to damage from oils in the future, or worse, leave a sticky residue that attracts more dirt.

For water-soluble stains, spot treat with white vinegar diluted with warm, but not hot, water. Pour a small amount over the stain and blot gently with white rags. When the surface dirt is completely gone, place several white rags over the spot and weight them down with a heavy object for a couple of hours. The cotton wicks the moisture from the carpet and helps prevent the pad from becoming saturated, thus avoiding the potential for mildew growth.

Oily stains are more difficult to remove. Use a small amount of dilute dish detergent and blot the stain. Remove as much moisture as possible, then follow with the vinegar solution to rinse any sticky, soapy residue, blotting and wetting until all traces of soap have been removed.

In each case, running a fan in the room for several hours after removing the weighted rags helps the area dry thoroughly. Vacuum after the carpet has dried to restore the texture. There is a chance the stain will wick to the surface and reappear and, if it does, simply repeat the process.

FOUR

Kitchen Patrol: Win the War Against Grease, Grime, and Unintentional Science Projects

Some call the kitchen the heart of a home. Whether you are a scratch cook or you assemble meals from boxes, the kitchen needs to be sanitary. If it's been a while since the kitchen has received a thorough cleaning, the first run through may be a little—OK quite—time consuming. This is the "I've just moved in," the "my mother-in-law is coming for the first white-glove inspection," the "I'm about to put the house on the market" clean. Put on some old clothes, find the rubber gloves, crank up some music, and get started.

Helpful tools to have on hand:

- Kitchen washcloth or sponge
- Old toothbrush and unwaxed dental floss
- Bar Keepers Friend
- Dish detergent such as Dawn (the plain, not fancy, kind)

Take Your Mind Off It

While cleaning, I dig listening to audiobooks and podcasts. They keep my mind busy when the work is mind numbing.

Cleaning A Light Fixture

Dear Home-Ec 101,

Is there an easy way to clean the light fixtures in my kitchen?

Signed,
Dim in Dulles

Before doing anything, turn off the power, preferably at the circuit. When it comes to things that shouldn't be mixed, water and electricity rank right up there with bleach and ammonia. Allow the light bulbs to cool before dismantling the fixture. Many times the light bulb has to be unscrewed to remove the decorative housing. If the sconce is glass, consider running it through the dishwasher. If it's crystal, you're better off caring for that delicate little flower by hand. Wipe down any metalwork or cords with a rag dampened with degreaser. Reassemble the entire fixture after the housing has dried. Frequent wipe downs with vinegar will prevent the need to take the whole thing apart in the future.

- Degreaser
- Chlorine bleach or other sanitizing agent
- Paper towels or an abundance of rags
- Vacuum cleaner with a soft-bristle attachment
- Bucket
- Rubber gloves
- Broom/dustpan/foxtail brush

The Sink

Start by emptying your sink. Pile all the dishes up on the counter, in a dishpan, wherever, but get them out of the sink. There are a couple of reasons for this. First, you need the sink, even if you're only going to rinse the dishes for the dishwasher. Second, it's a mental trick. (Look at that! Something has been accomplished.) Use that positive reinforcement to move on to the next task.

Now that the sink is empty, clean it. If your sink is solid surface—stainless steel or porcelain—scrub away any stuck-on bits of food using a mild abrasive powder such as Bar Keepers Friend, baking powder, or salt on any stains. Use a toothbrush and dental floss to get behind the faucet.*

Most faucets come equipped with an aerator, which increases the water pressure by forcing the water through a screen. If you have hard water, this screen becomes clogged with mineral deposits. Improving your water pressure may be as simple as cleaning the screen. Most of these screens can be removed from the faucet without any tools. Wear rubber gloves, only to improve your grip. Grasp the tip of the faucet and twist to the left. If the unit is too tight to remove by hand, use pliers with the jaws inserted into a rubber glove. (The glove prevents scratching the finish.) Once disassembled, use a toothbrush and hot, soapy water to scrub the pieces. Soak the screen in white vinegar to remove any mineral buildup. Reassemble the faucet, give it a good wipe down, and admire your handiwork.

Once the sink has been tackled, load the dishwasher—if you have one—and finish washing any remaining dishes by hand. This is often the hardest step. Wash *all* of the dishes, and put *all* of the dishes away. Congratulations, your sink and dishes are now clean.

Confession

My sink is similar to Corian and it attracts stains like crazy. If I wave a coffee pot over it, brown splotches appear. I hate it and am actually dreaming of the day I can replace it with stainless.

---

* If I had been in charge of the world's faucet design, under no circumstances would sinks have a gap too small for a toothbrush to fit between the faucet and lip of the sink; unfortunately, no one asked.

Microwave

Fill a microwave-safe bowl with three parts water and one part white vinegar (1½ cups water, ½ cup vinegar). Microwave the bowl with the vinegar water on high for three minutes. Leave the door closed for an additional five minutes. The steam will soften some of the crusty food splatters. Always be careful of burns when using this technique.

While you're waiting for the steam to work, move on to the cabinets. After five minutes, wipe out the microwave with a dishcloth or sponge. If there are still some crusty bits, repeat the vinegar-water trick. If it has been ages since the appliance has been cleaned, it may take several repetitions.

Superheating in the Microwave

Never use the microwave to boil plain water, as there is a risk of superheating the liquid. If this happens, simply bumping the bowl can cause it to boil with excessive force, resulting in a potential burn hazard.

Cabinets

If you cook without running the range hood,** steam and grease released during the cooking process float all over the kitchen and gleefully attach to the walls and cabinets. If your cabinets have decorative ridges, as many do, grab the vacuum and use the soft bristle attachment on the ridges. Work from the top left of the room to the bottom right. This drill will become familiar. It took many years for me to accept this step as a necessary part of cleaning, but it prevents the maddening transfer of pet hair or random fuzzies from one cabinet to the next during the upcoming degreasing stage.

Despite its acidic nature, diluted white vinegar is typically a useful and green degreaser and disinfectant, but if it has been a long time since the

---

** In many homes, this appliance is referred to as "that noisy fan thingy."

Dirt on White Cabinets

If you have Obsessive Compulsive Disorder (OCD) and have white painted cabinets—an unholy combination if I do say so—cotton swabs dipped in isopropyl (rubbing) alcohol can get most of the dirt from a tight corner. Use this technique sparingly as it takes a small amount of paint with it.

kitchen has seen a serious cleaning, either compromise your vow to forever be kind to the environment and break out the big guns, or get ready to tone your arms as you apply the necessary elbow grease.

Again, work from left to right, top to bottom using a damp rag, sponge, or soft-bristled brush, and gently scrub each cabinet door. To prevent damage to exposed wood, dry each cabinet as you make your way around the room. Unless the home was built with a high-end kitchen, assume the cabinets are made of MDF or pressboard, a less-expensive substitute for wood. It is also quite susceptible to water damage.*

Shelves and Drawers

As we continue our top-down clean, it's time to hit the shelves and drawers. If the shelves need cleaning, unload only one at a time. Wipe the shelf with the degreasing solution, rinse, dry, and return the items to their proper places. Remember, the more items hanging out on a horizontal surface, the more clutter will be drawn to the area.

I'm ambivalent about using liner paper or mats on shelves. That said, I do use a liner mat for shelves that hold drinking glasses and mugs. All other shelves just get wiped down from time to time. The mats I use are the ones that can be washed in hot, soapy water and then rinsed. Because drinking glasses should be stored upside down, I prefer a sanitary surface.

* If the paint or protective coating cracks, be prepared to wake up one day and find your kitchen doing its best impression of the Elephant Man.

Built-up Grease on Cabinets

Dear Home-Ec 101,

We recently moved into our home. I'm not sure, but I think it was home to a herd of frat boys on the Atkins diet. The walls and cabinets are covered with cooking grease. The cabinets are early tract house circa 1980s, MDF with veneer. What can I do to de-gross the kitchen until we can save up for a remodel?

Signed,
Animal House

I'm convinced whomever invented MDF (or pressboard) signed a pact with the devil. This cheap wood substitute has caused many a homeowner to gnash her teeth. You must be extremely careful when cleaning any furnishing made of compressed wood, as the introduction of water causes the wood fibers to swell.

In most cases, I recommend using white vinegar as an environmentally friendly option, but there are times where a more powerful option is needed. Old grease stains would require a vinegar user a lot of scrubbing and repeat applications to remove the buildup. With each attempt, more water has an opportunity to seep into nicks and cracks, increasing the chance of permanently damaging the MDF. Therefore, in cases like this, I recommend a strong degreaser such as Lestoil. Use gloves, as the degreaser will remove the oil from your skin. When you apply degreaser to the rag, wring it out before you even think of approaching the cabinets.

Drawers are excellent for hiding clutter, but they also excel at catching dust, crumbs, and hair. Empty the drawers one at a time. As you empty each drawer, get rid of all the random junk that has accumulated. Yes, it's good to have one or two bread ties on hand, but do you really need forty-two? Check pens to make sure they work, enter phone numbers into your

Scuff Marks on Cabinets

Dear Home-Ec 101,

My kitchen features a breakfast bar; I love this! What I don't love is that the painted cabinets under the breakfast bar now feature scuff marks. Can I remove these, or must I face repainting every few months?

Signed,
Scuffed in Scuttsburg

Any of the cleaning sponges made from melamine foam should work like a charm. It's important to remember, whichever brand you choose, that these "sponges" act as a mild abrasive. If you rub too hard, it's possible to take off some of the paint along with the scuff. On the upside, the eraser may buff out some of the tiny nicks that love to catch and hang onto dirt.

contact list, sharpen pencils before they get put away, toss expired coupons. Once the drawer is empty, use the vacuum's soft bristle attachment to suck up the hair and crumbs. Then give the drawer a good wipe with degreaser, dry, and return the contents.

Appliances

Clean the range. Save cleaning the oven for a time when the kitchen can be aired out. Wipe down the outside of all appliances. Don't forget the top of the refrigerator.

While we're giving the kitchen a deep clean, consider vacuuming your refrigerator coils. This energy-saving step should be performed a couple times a year. To reduce the risk of shock, either unplug the fridge or flip the circuit breaker. The location of your appliance's coils depends on the age of your refrigerator. On some older models the coils can be reached by removing the kick plate on the front of the appliance, just beneath the doors. This may either snap out of place or may be secured with screws. Once removed, take it outside or into the shower and spray off the dust bunnies and their spawn. If yours is particularly grimy, use degreaser to help break up the film; allow the kick plate to dry.

To vacuum the coils themselves, gently insert the wand attachment into the space usually covered by the kick plate. Suck out as much grime as possible. Some companies sell specialized attachments that have bristles solely for this purpose, but I believe those to be unnecessary. Replace the kick plate when you have finished. Never shove the wand forcefully under your appliance. Doing so might knock parts loose.

There are two other possible locations for the coils. Carefully pull the refrigerator away from the wall. Always move the fridge straight in and straight out to minimize damage to the flooring. The coils will either be exposed on the back of the appliance or behind a kick plate. If the coils are exposed, simply vacuum any dust with the vacuum's soft bristle attachment. Alternatively, if the coils are extremely grimy, use a rag dampened with degreaser or white vinegar. (This is why we unplugged the appliance.) If the coils are not exposed, use a wrench or screwdriver to remove the screws.

Once the plate has been removed, use the soft bristled vacuum tool to remove any built-up dust. Replace the cover, sweep or vacuum up any debris, and carefully push the appliance back into place. Be sure not to pinch any electrical cords or water lines. Restore power to the unit by either resetting the breaker or plugging in the unit. This project should take less than ten minutes start to finish, if it is performed on a regular basis.

Stainless Steel

Use degreaser solution to wipe down all of the remaining appliances except for the stainless steel ones. If you have stainless steel, use plain dish detergent (one that contains no additives such as bleach) in hot water. Wipe down each appliance to remove any greasy buildup, then rinse with plain

Countertop Stains

Dear Home-Ec 101,

The other day, I placed a wet receipt on a laminate counter to dry. It was one of those old-fashioned ones with purple ink. The next morning, I discovered I'd put it ink-side down and now had a nice copy of the receipt on the countertop. Everything I tried lightened the stain but did not remove all traces. I did try one of those magic erasers, but it didn't seem to affect it at all. I'm wondering if you have any other ideas for me?

Signed,
I said I wanted a copy of the receipt, but this is ridiculous!

I have been in your shoes before. The ink has crept into tiny cracks and crevices on your seemingly smooth counter. I would first try dabbing only the ink with isopropyl (rubbing) alcohol. It won't always work, but it's a great solvent for removing some types of ink. Use care with isopropyl alcohol and test an inconspicuous location, as materials may vary. If the isopropyl alcohol doesn't do the trick, it's time to pull out our old pal, Bar Keepers Friend, a mild scouring powder made from oxacylic acid. Of course you will want to test this in an inconspicuous area as well. Make a paste and spread it over the stain, then give it a few minutes to work before wiping with a damp rag. Use a back-and-forth motion to rub out the mark and cautiously apply a little elbow grease, but be careful not to rub out your design.

water, and dry with a chamois to remove fingerprints. You can use olive oil to help repel fingerprints on stainless steel, but be aware this may darken the appliance over time. This is also the case with many commercially available stainless steel cleaners. They all have an oil-based ingredient that can build up over time.

Countertops

Attack laminate countertops with your degreaser of choice. Work from left to right, moving small appliances and knickknacks as you progress through the room. If your kitchen has solid-surface countertops such as Corian, marble, or granite, use special care. A 50:50 mixture of isopropyl (rubbing) alcohol and water is a great degreaser for granite, and Bar Keepers Friend works well to remove stains from solid-surface counters. Never use acidic cleaners of any type on marble. Soapstone counters should be washed with soapy water, dried, then treated with food-grade mineral oil. Just like we swore with the oath, always test any cleaner in an inconspicuous area and never use any chemical that may void a manufacturer's warranty.

Food Preparation Surfaces

Food preparation surfaces, whether countertops or cutting boards, require a two-step cleaning process. First use hot, soapy water to remove any dirt, soil, or grime, then follow with a sanitizing spray of diluted chlorine bleach. Create this sanitizing spray by mixing 1 tablespoon of chlorine bleach into 1 gallon of water. Spray onto the surface to be sanitized and allow it to sit for several minutes before wiping dry.

Toe Boards and Floors

You're almost done. Use a rag or a foxtail brush to clean the toe boards—that's the under-the-cabinet facing used to cover seams and joists, making the piece look like a solid unit. It's difficult to sweep under cabinets, so this is often a very dirty job. Brush away the debris and then wipe with your degreasing solution. Performing this task with some regularity helps ensure pests don't make themselves comfortable in your home.

Now it's time to sweep and mop. These chores are outlined in chapter 3 on flooring. When you're done, fix yourself a drink and admire your handiwork. Just be sure to rinse out your glass and put it in the dishwasher.

Caring for Butcher's Block

Dear Home-Ec 101,

I recently inherited a lovely butcher's block table, but I have no idea how to care for it.

Signed,
The Butcher's Ex

Sandpaper, meet Ms. Ex. Ms. Ex, meet sandpaper, fine grit of course. If you have no idea how this butcher's block was cared for, it's important to strip the surface before using it to prepare food. Start with 80-grit sandpaper and sand the surface, then wipe with a damp, clean rag. This brings up the nap of the wood. Next, sand the surface again, this time with 100-grit sandpaper, wipe, and if you want you can work your way up as high as 200-grit (this is up to you). Once you have sanded the surface to your preference, break out the food-grade mineral oil or a combination of four parts food-grade mineral oil and one part beeswax, gently heated until they can be mixed. You can heat this in a double boiler or one of those itty-bitty slow cookers made for dips.

Wipe the entire surface of your butcher's block table, let it cure for at least 20 minutes, and then buff away the excess. Repeat this the following day and your table is ready to use as a food preparation surface. Once a month or so, re-treat the surface with either food-grade mineral oil or the combination of oil and wax. Between treatments, simply clean the wood with soap and water. You may also use lemon juice and salt to scrub away any stains. If your table has come in contact with raw meat or poultry, use a weak bleach solution after using soap and water. Dry the surface and treat with food-grade mineral oil.

Milk Stains on Wood

Dear Home-Ec 101,

How does one remove dried milk from wood? Every low surface in my kitchen (chair legs, table legs, cabinets) is full of dried milk spots from spills that always go farther and cover more area than you can initially see. No matter how I try to clean them, I get the same result: It looks clean while it's still wet and I think I've won, but as soon as it dries, the spots are still all there!

Signed,
Sobbing Suze in Toddler Town

Quit crying, the solution isn't that difficult. Grab a bucket, or two if you're lazy like me and hate getting up and down from the floor. If you take the two-bucket approach, you may as well grab two rags. Fill the first bucket with a healthy dollop of dish soap, something like old-fashioned Dawn—the plain, dark blue, nothing-fancy-added dish detergent. Add just an inch or two of water. Now, swish the water until you have a lot of frothy suds. Fill your other bucket with clear, hot water.

Wet the first rag with just the soapy bubbles; don't dip it down into the water. The world won't end if you do, but try to get it as soapy, with just the foam, as possible. Now scrub off the milk spots and use a little elbow grease while you are at it. Next, take your second rag, dip it in the plain water, wring it out, and wipe off the soap. Be sure to rinse this rag frequently.

When the chair legs are dry, give them a polish. I'm not huge on recommending brands, but I am a fan of Method's Wood for Good. While I'm usually not a fan of scented products, it smells amazing.

FIVE

The Great Bathroom Cleansing: Tubs, Toilets, and Rubber Gloves

The bathroom, the loo, the WC: It doesn't matter what it's called, it must be cleaned, and frequently at that.* So, what do you do? Suck it up and plow in.

Declutter

First remove all clothes, towels, and washcloths that are strewn about. Perhaps you're the sort of person who never, ever lets dirty clothes go anywhere but the hamper. Or perhaps you're like all my family members who like to drop their clothing right next to, or better yet, on top of, but not in the hamper. Either way, if there is clothing in the bathroom, remove it.

Next, discard all trash in the bathroom. I normally empty the bathroom trash every week on trash day, but somehow little bits of trash tend to end up in odd places, like underneath cabinets and behind the toilet. I don't always get those on trash day, so I gather up all the flotsam plus all the trash in the trash can, and take it out. If you do not use a liner in your trash can,

---

* There is, of course, always the option of moving, but good luck finding a buyer if you're leaving due to a fear of a little labor. Throw in the cost of litigation for abandoning multiple properties over the years and the idea begins to lose some of its appeal.

empty it and set it in the tub, fill it partially with hot water and a healthy dollop of vinegar. Let that soak for a few minutes while the vinegar does its deodorizing magic.

Now, clear off your sink area; yes, even the stuff that belongs there. We're not cleaning the vanity at this point, just clearing the stage. Place all toiletry items in the cabinet or out in the hall. With a clear work space, there's no need to worry about accidentally spraying the toothbrushes with glass cleaner or worse.

Cleaning Overhead

Light Fixtures

Look up at the light fixtures. Will a brief dusting do the job or are the sconces fuzzy? If they are filthy, a combination of humidity, dust, and possibly hair spray has created a stubborn layer of grime. I like to let the dishwasher do the dirty work on the glass globes or plastic covers—top rack only with no detergent—but those made with other materials need to be handled more carefully. Use a rag dampened with degreaser to wipe metal sconces and frames. Isopropyl (rubbing) alcohol is also an option for metal sconces, unless they have been painted with acrylic or latex paint.

Corners and Exhaust Fans

Turn the lights back on and take a good look at the corners where the wall meets the ceiling. Cobwebs? But of course. No problem, wrap the head of a broom in an old pillowcase and work your way around the room. Gently

Cool Your Bulbs

Always turn off the power and allow light bulbs to cool before cleaning a light fixture. Hot light bulb + moisture = KAPOW! This is in addition to the usual formula where water + electricity = yikes!

Use Ventilation

Bathroom fans aren't only good for privacy. Run the fan during and for fifteen minutes after showers. Doing this significantly reduces the amount of moisture in the air, making your bathroom less hospitable for mold, bacteria, and fungus.

wipe away the cobwebs. While you have the broom in your hand, take a look at the exhaust fan. Give it a gentle swipe to knock down any dust bunnies.

If you've never cleaned the fan, it may be time to break out the stepladder and unscrew the cover. Be careful, I don't know why, but bugs seem to enjoy crawling up there to die. Suppress the squeals and shudders (you're on a stepladder and balance is important), dispose of the bugs, and wipe down the slats with a rag dampened with degreaser. Reattach the fan cover.

Sweep the Floors

Then vacuum or sweep the floor and the bottom of your completely dry tub/shower. Never vacuum wet surfaces unless your vacuum is specifically designed to do so. This concludes the somewhat dry portion of your bathroom cleaning experience. It's time to get wet.

We will now be messing with some chemicals, so either open the window or turn on the exhaust fan. If neither is an option, use an oscillating or box fan to pull fresh air into the room. Even when using fairly green products such as isopropyl (rubbing) alcohol, it is important to understand that the fumes can still be harmful.

The Toilet, Preview

Flush the toilet; I'm not kidding. If you use bleach to clean your toilet, the bleach could react with the ammonia in urine. I told you these chemicals show up in annoying places, remember? While bleach is generally a great sanitizing solution, it's not the best for cleaning a toilet. Urine contains dissolved salts that remain on surfaces even after the liquid has evaporated. If there are males in the household, it's important to remember that like any other liquid, pee splashes. The ammonium salts left behind are responsible for a lot of bathroom funk and odor. When it comes to removing these alkaline salts, acids are your best bet. As a bonus, acids also remove hard water scaling. If it has been a long time since your toilet has received any attention, one of the thicker commercial cleaners may be helpful. If you go this route, there are environmentally friendly alternatives made from citric acid. Even the most environmentally friendly toilet cleaner will have a label describing the content as an irritant.*

Shower and Bathtub

While the toilet cleaner does its magic, it is time to tackle the shower and the bathtub. Step into your shower and look at the showerhead. If the holes are clogged with limescale, gather a plastic bag, a large rubber band, and white vinegar. Fill the bag partway with white vinegar, then place the bag around the showerhead and fasten the bag in place with the rubber band. The nozzle should be submerged. The acidity of the vinegar will loosen the limescale. Leave the bag up there until you have finished cleaning the bathroom.

It's important to choose the best cleaner for your bathroom fixtures, as common household cleaners can damage the materials used to make tubs and showers. Use care when choosing cleaners for acrylic, glass, and fiberglass, as all of these materials can be scratched by abrasive cleaners. Not all abrasive cleaners leave visible scratches, but dirt, soap scum, and hard water deposits all find their way into those tiny crevices, fogging glass and leaving a dingy residue. Acidic cleaners all work well for these surfaces, dissolving the minerals and breaking the bonds of soap. Shower curtains can be taken down and thrown into the washing machine on gentle with vinegar or borax.

* Take off the tinfoil hat—even vinegar and lemon juice are irritants. If you squirted either in your eyes, they would be irritated.

Soap Scum

Soap scum is a big problem for those who live in areas with hard water. The high concentration of minerals in the water become surrounded by soap molecules that stick to the walls and sides of tubs and showers. Limescale is similar, but involves only the hard water minerals, and is equally obnoxious.

The nice thing about using the washing machine is that the spin cycle makes the whole ordeal less of a drippy pain. Before you get started, you must find the cleaner compatible with your bathroom surfaces. Here's the rundown.

Acrylic Tubs and Showers

These units are also referred to as plastic or gel-coated fiberglass. All of these surfaces are easily scratched and should be cared for in the same manner. Use gentle soap, such as dish soap with no additives, or even baby shampoo. Dishwasher detergent may be too harsh and could chemically etch (scratch) the surface, just as using an abrasive pad could. Small nicks and scratches will eventually cause the surface to look dull and give ring around the tub a jump start. Simple ring around the bathtub can be removed with a mixture of equal parts white vinegar and water, which is also useful for removing soap scum. Never use an abrasive cleaner on these surfaces, and take particular care if using a scouring powder. These vary by brand and a picture of a tub on the label does not mean it is safe for all of the materials used to build tubs or showers. It is possible to refinish a worn tub or shower pan, but it is a labor-intensive job and won't always be a perfect match. Dirt does damage. It's important to remove it frequently to maintain the quality of your fixture's finish.

Porcelain

Many older homes have tubs made of porcelain over cast iron. Porcelain is an incredibly hard surface and is quite durable, but it has a drawback.

Dealing with Tub Funk

Dear Home-Ec 101,

My bathtub is so funky, it makes James Brown look stodgy—especially because he's dead, but I digress. The yuck in my tub is so nasty, I'm afraid to take a shower, and my co-workers are starting to complain. Help me, Home-Ec 101, you're my only hope!

Signed,

Princess Leia

Sometimes life gets away from everyone. The filth can come off in the same way it went on, a little at a time. Grab an old nylon pouf and a little shampoo. Face your fear and take a shower. While you're in there, scrub one side; the next time you shower, scrub another side. There is no rule that says you have to clean the tub in one go.

However, if you need to get a running start on a bad mess, try filling the tub with hot water and adding one or two scoops of laundry detergent. Allow this to soak several hours or overnight. (Skip the soaking technique if there are young children present in the home; it's never worth the effort saved to create a hazard.) The enzymes in the detergent can help bring the body oil into solution, which will make tomorrow's application of cleaner more effective.

If your tub is porcelain, use vinegar and water. If it's acrylic, make a paste of baking soda and water and scrub the sides and bottom of the tub. Rinse well and dry.

Porcelain and enamel can chip from a hard blow, and the chips are, for all practical purposes, permanent damage. Due to its durability, many household cleaners can be used, but to play it safe, always rinse the tub after using an acidic cleaner. Over time, the careless application of acidic cleaners can damage the surface of the tub.

Ring around the tub easily wipes away from porcelain tubs with iso-propyl (rubbing) alcohol. If the ring is old and set, dishwasher detergent applied as a paste can be quite effective. For rust stains (these often occur in areas with hard water), chlorine bleach is useless. Try a product specifically designed for the problem such as CLR. Though porcelain is very durable, avoid harsh abrasives.

Tile

Tile, or more specifically the grout filling the gaps between the tiles, needs special care. Most grout needs to be treated periodically with a sealant to protect it from stains. Most tile used in bathrooms is sealed. A quick test is to place a drop of water on dry grout. If it darkens, it is unsealed or the surface has been damaged over time. In either case it needs to be cleaned thoroughly and resealed to prevent damage.

Due to its nature, glazed ceramic tile is stain resistant. The glazing process creates a strong, smooth finish. It is the grout that creates the biggest headache for homeowners. When choosing a cleaning product for everyday use, ensure that it is pH neutral, which means it is neither acidic nor alkaline (base). Acidic cleaners can damage the surface of tile over time, etching the surface and creating rough areas for dirt, soap scum, and mineral deposits from hard water to cling. Acidic cleaners are especially damaging to the grout; they eat away at the material itself, much like acid rain slowly dissolves statues. After each shower, use a squeegee to wipe away excess water. A few seconds of daily prevention is more effective than cleaning after damage has occurred. If the grout has become stained, use only an alkaline household cleaner and gently scrub with a soft bristled brush. Always rinse tile after cleaning and squeegee dry. Grout may need to be resealed periodically, as the sealant can break down with exposure to mild acids and normal wear and tear. When this happens, stains seep into the grout, making removal difficult. If the grout has become stained, try using 3 percent hydrogen peroxide on the stain before rinsing, drying, and resealing.

Dear Home-Ec 101,

I've heard I should wax my tub to keep it shiny. Are they just yanking my chain or what? Wax on? Wax off?

Signed,

Ms. Macchio

If you have ever searched the Internet for tips on cleaning bathroom or kitchen fixtures, you are bound to find the suggestion to use wax as a means to restore shine and reduce soap scum buildup. Is this a reliable tip? Well, yes and no. Like most things on the Internet, there is a lot of truth to the suggestion, but its effectiveness depends on what you have to work with. If your tub is a million years old, with chipped and scarred porcelain, there is really only so much that can be done, and most of it involves cleaning regularly and not stressing over what can't be changed in between. If the tub is newer and only needs a little love, waxing will work brilliantly.

I suggest using carnauba wax, a plant-derived wax (check the automotive section for this wax). It won't create a diamond finish, but it eliminates the worry of coming into contact with excessive and unnecessary chemicals. Second, never wax the bottom of any fixture, tub, or shower; doing so increases the chances of slips and falls. Speaking as a full-time klutz, I do not need this risk increased. Waxing works by filling in tiny nicks and cracks. Without a toehold, the lime and soap scum have no place to build up. I wouldn't wax the tub with every cleaning, but you'll need to reapply from time to time.

If soap scum has built up enough that an alkaline cleaner and elbow grease are not enough to fix the problem, try using diluted isopropyl (rubbing) alcohol. It may be necessary to resort to an acidic cleaner such as

Dear Home-Ec 101,

Help! I've got funky stuff coming out of my jetted tub. I turned it on the other night and bits of black sludge ruined my bath. How do I clean out the jets? What is it, anyway?

Signed,
Jetty Betty

Readers always get mad at me for telling them nasty things about their homes. Do you really want to know what that sludge is? Each time you bathe and use the jets, bits of skin, body oil, dirt, and soap are left in the jet; this moist environment is heaven for microorganisms. The sludge is a result of their hedonistic lifestyle—eating, reproducing, excreting—in your jet lines. Nasty.

Once a month, fill the tub with hot water just high enough to operate the jets, add between ½ cup and 1 cup of dishwasher detergent and run the jets for ten to twenty minutes. Some manufacturers recommend adding ½ cup of bleach to the water, but use caution if you have a septic system. The dishwasher detergent should be sufficient to clear the lines of the bacteria's food supply; no food, no parties. In this case, there really isn't anything to be done about the moist environment short of never using the tub, and that defeats the purpose. Drain the tub, wipe away that lovely bathtub ring, and refill with cold water to rinse out the lines. Run the tub for a few minutes, drain, and get ready to soak without inviting millions of your one-celled friends.

white vinegar and water. Use extreme caution to prevent damage to the tile and grout. Apply the mixture, scrub with a soft bristled brush, and rinse thoroughly. Work in small sections, rinsing as you go to minimize damage from the acidic cleaner.

Marble

Many of the same cleaning recommendations for tile hold true for marble. Never use an acidic cleaner on marble. While it seems as though marble is a hard surface, acid can damage the surface. To clean marble and granite, I suggest using isopropyl (rubbing) alcohol and water *or* a cleaner recommended by the manufacturer of the fixture.

Glass Shower Doors

A mixture of equal parts water and white vinegar can be sprayed on shower doors after each use at very little cost. After spraying, squeegee the doors and you'll never face soap scum and hard water deposits. Some home owners go as far as Rain-X-ing their shower doors. If the idea piques your interest, be my guest.

Caulk

Mold and mildew love caulk and while bleach kills mold, the water left behind after the sodium chlorate has evaporated provides a nice damp home for new spores to take root. Both white vinegar and isopropyl (rubbing) alcohol are effective at inhibiting mold growth. Isopropyl (rubbing) alcohol is a solvent, but it is pH neutral. Choose your weapon according to the surrounding materials, as the cleaner may come into contact with these surfaces. Caulking is a relatively straightforward do-it-yourself project, and with a little preparation, most people are up to the task. Don't be afraid of recaulking every few years.

Vanities and Mirrors

Next up, things that need to be sprayed and wiped. Bathroom sinks and counters are filth magnets—toothpaste to the left, shaving cream to the right,* makeup, hair products, and stray hair between. It can get nasty,

---

* Stuck in the middle with you!

Fog-Free Mirrors

After cleaning the mirror, try this simple trick to make it temporarily fog free. Apply a small amount of shaving cream to a paper towel or rag. Use the rag to polish the mirror. It takes a little elbow grease, but the steam from the shower won't be able to cling to the mirror as easily. Neat.

quick. To make things easier, scrape or wipe away as much grime as possible before adding cleaning products to the party. A flat, nylon scraper* can come in handy when trying to remove hardened toothpaste or scraping remnants from the soap ledge. It makes no sense to use a chemical to remove what can be accomplished with a simple wipe or scrape. Once the big chunks are gone, it's time to tackle the mirror.

Use whatever floats your boat: isopropyl (rubbing) alcohol, water and vinegar, or even commercial glass cleaner. You're the boss, wield your power wisely and mind your overspray. Some cleaning products can strip the color from paint or wallpaper, and remember isopropyl (rubbing) alcohol damages latex paint.

Notice we have stepped back into the whole clean-from-the-top-down idea. Surprise, there was a method to this madness.

Next up, the vanity. Remember our rules from the kitchen? Use the appropriate cleaner for whatever material comprises your vanity. For laminate counters use a standard degreaser; use isopropyl (rubbing) alcohol and water on marble or granite; and enamel is tough, inert, and forgiving.**

Don't forget to clean behind and under your faucet and around the plunger for the sink plug. Seriously, take a look, it's nasty. Dental floss,

---

* I get invited to a lot of those home demonstration product parties, and theses scrapers are my standby, guilt-induced order. Usually they are under five-dollars and I ordered something, so back off.

** Completely unlike the author.

Stains in the Shower

Dear Home-Ec 101,

We keep getting these pale pinkish stains on the shower curtains and at the base of the tub. Our neighbor has the same issue, and he thinks it's metal in our water supply. Could it be mold? I've found a weak bleach solution or most any bath cleaner completely fades the stains without much scrubbing—but the spots will return in less than a week if I don't spray on a near-daily basis.

Signed,
Pretty in Pink

You are right on target cleaning with a weak bleach solution. The microorganism behind your bathroom cleaning quandary is Serratia marcescens, and it loves damp environments. Interestingly, the bacteria were once used for experimentation due to their coloration, which made it easy to track growth, even without a microscope. However, the bacteria have been found to cause urinary tract infections and, rarely, pneumonia.

Chlorine is an effective preventative and will wipe it out temporarily. Unfortunately, chlorine evaporates more quickly than water, and eventually the airborne bacteria will reproduce in sufficient numbers to create the pink stain in showers, and in toilets that are used infrequently. Remember to periodically clean your showerhead if you notice the telltale pink discoloration.

toothpicks, or an old toothbrush—not your spouse's, just don't go there—work well for this job. Glass cleaner is great for getting rid of water spots on a stainless steel faucet.

The Toilet: Scrub Down

Back to the toilet! I know, the cleaning tutorial you've waited for your entire life. Because an acidic cleaner is working in the bowl, be sure to use an acidic cleaner, such as vinegar and water, for the exterior. Once again, the top-to-bottom approach serves us well. If it has been a while since the toilet has been cleaned, be prepared to use several rags or paper towels.

Begin by applying your cleaning spray to your rag, then wipe the top of the tank, followed by the sides. Next, clean the topside of the lid, followed by the underside. Next, wipe the seat itself. I usually spray the seat with a vinegar solution, wipe it, then lift, spray, and wipe the underside. Before tackling the rim and behind the seat, it's time for the bowl scrubbing. Set your dirty rags in a bucket or on the floor if you are prepared to mop. Do not place these on your clean counter.

Wield your toilet brush, assume the position, and scrub any visible stains around the water line. Next, raise the brush and scrub the underside of the rim to remove any stains from hard water or that nasty pink mold that grows in wet spaces. Flush while the brush is still in the bowl to rinse away the cleaner. Give the brush another few swishes to ensure it's clean and return it to its stand or holder.

Back to wiping, next up is the rim. Any cleaner that has splashed up from the bowl will make this job easier. Remember, it's just cleaner and water from the bowl, not actual body fluids, don't be a baby; hands wash. Once the rim is clean, lower both the lid and the seat and pay special attention to the

Smelly Shower

Dear Home-Ec 101,

I have this nasty smell in my bathroom. It is very hard for me to describe; I think I have it pinpointed to the shower stall. I have totally scrubbed it. It is so bad, I worry that everyone can smell it! I noticed it is very bad right after we shower, too. Do you have any idea what this is and how to get rid of it?!

Signed,
Desperate in Dayton

Oh, the mystery funk has vexed many home owners. One at a time, run the sink, fill the tub, and flush the toilet closest to the affected shower. Listen for any gurgling sounds. If you hear noises, it is possible that your drain is partially clogged. Check chapter 14 for directions on clearing a clogged drain.

If you are absolutely sure that there is no clog in the drain, you must make your landlord aware of the problem. If you are a home owner you should call the water and sewer company. Sometimes problems develop in the sewage lines, and a foul odor can be indicative of this. They will send someone out to perform a smoke test. During this test, the sewage lines are filled with smoke, which rises. If there are any leaks, smoke will show up where it doesn't belong or it won't escape through the sewer vent pipes.

area between the hinge and the tank. It doesn't matter how it arrives; all that matters is that it goes. And look at that, we've arrived at the most dreaded portion of the task. It's time to get on your hands and knees and clean the outside of the bowl and the sides. It's the same as cleaning the tank, just with more nooks and crannies. If you knock off one of the bolt covers, don't stress, they snap right back into place.

Finally, sweep, mop, and make sure those rags make it to the laundry.

SIX

Dining Rooms and Dusty Dens of Doom: Yes, You Do Windows

Living and dining rooms seem to develop a cluttered, lived-in look at the drop of a hat. Well, that's true for mine, maybe you're special. The good news is giving these rooms a deep clean is usually much easier than either the kitchen or the bathrooms. There are exceptions for those who keep extensive collections of figurines out in the open and line every surface with fake plants, but in my mind, these people are asking for painstaking dusting sessions. The tools needed for the living room and dining room vary, depending on whether they are carpeted, heavily furnished, or laid out to display tchotchkes.

Clear the Clutter

The first thing to do is to clear the clutter that doesn't belong. Don't get distracted; if you're like me, and have a hard time focusing on the task at hand, grab a large basket and set it just outside the doorway. All items that need to be put away in other rooms go there (putting these items away is a great task for children or other unpaid laborers). Limiting the trips out of the room keeps the old ADD in check. Without a convenient excuse, I can't head down the rabbit trail of "oh, I'll just start a load of laundry while I'm in here" or "oh look, this floor needs to be swept."*

Dust Overhead

Once the clutter has been cleared, it's back to the top-to-bottom, left-to-right system. Pick a corner of the room as your starting point; now look up toward the ceiling, are there cobwebs? How did I know? If you have a low ceiling, the soft bristle attachment of your vacuum cleaner should work well. For higher ceilings, use the broom-in-the-pillowcase trick from chapter 5. Don't swing for the fences, you could take out a window.

Seasonal Spins

In cooler months, ceiling fans should slowly spin in a clockwise direction. This gently forces the warm air downward when it would rather lurk about near the rafters. In the summer, the fan should turn counterclockwise with hurricane force; this creates a distraction from the actual temperature.

Whether you have a chandelier, recessed lighting, or a ceiling fixture, the lighting unit is going to collect dust. Make sure the power is off before disassembling the fixture. Clear or frosted glass shades or plastic covers can be washed on the top rack of the dishwasher with no detergent. Do not use the dishwasher if the covers have gilded edges or metallic rims. In those cases it's best to wash by hand with a mild dish soap. Use a feather duster or a rag dampened slightly with degreaser to wipe any chains or metalwork. Do not turn the power back on until the fixture has been reassembled.

* It's a lot like the children's classic *If You Give a Mouse a Cookie,* only less entertaining.

Ceiling fans are included in the light fixture category. The blades of a ceiling fan pick up an obscene amount of dust in relatively short periods of time. Dry dusting, followed by a degreaser, is usually enough to fix the fuzz balls. If your fan has painted blades, check to make sure the degreaser won't damage the paint by wiping the top side of the blade first. While you are up there, make sure your fan spins in the proper direction. Typically, the direction of the motor is changed by a small switch on the same part of the fan as the pull chain.

Window Coverings

Continuing the top-down approach, check out the windows and window coverings. A hundred years ago there was a difference between curtains and drapes, now it's mostly a matter of semantics and how formally the room is decorated. Basically, if you feel like being fancy and the curtains reach the floor, go ahead and call them drapes. Decorators, and those who want to be, can get quite uppity about their terms, but for our purposes, window coverings fall into a few categories:

Not all damage can be undone. Sometimes we can embrace the damage and call it a patina, which gives possessions character. If in doubt, check with someone who has trustworthy judgment.

window treatments (also valances and cornices), drapes/curtains, sheers, shades or blinds. Each one requires slightly different techniques for cleaning. Due to the variety of materials and decorations used to make drapes and fabric window treatments, dirt prevention is the best approach to extending the life of your decorations. If a window treatment, valance, or cornice is permanently attached to a wall fixture, you have two options to remove dust—vacuuming or using compressed air. Grease and dust will cause damage if they are allowed to build up on fabric.

Some drapes and curtains can be washed. Those assembled with hope and hot glue cannot. Use caution if no care tag is present and never wash drapes with trim, pleating, or ornaments in a washing machine, as they may be permanently damaged. Custom draperies may need to be professionally cleaned, but with regular dusting and vacuuming, this should be an infrequent occurrence. Sheers are the flimsy, almost see-through light curtains drawn for privacy rather than their ability to reduce drafts or block sunlight. These are machine washable in cold water on the gentle cycle. Be aware that all material has a particular life span, and strong sunlight weakens fibers. Be prepared to occasionally replace curtains and sheers as they fade or become sun damaged. You can reduce the amount of damage caused by sunlight by choosing lined curtains and drapes.

Blinds, whether wood, plastic, or metal, need frequent dusting. Plastic miniblinds can be taken down and soaked in a bathtub with dish soap. Use the shower to rinse the blinds thoroughly before allowing them to drip dry. Standard blinds and shutters, whether made from wood or man-made materials, should be vacuumed and then wiped with a—wait for it—rag dampened with degreaser. Rolling shades should be gently wiped with mildly soapy water, rinsed, and allowed to dry fully before retracting.

Windows

Anyone who has worn glasses is familiar with the, "why didn't I clean my glasses ages ago" sensation, and windows are the eyes of a home. If it has been a while since the windows have been washed, be prepared to be startled by the difference. Before starting on the glass itself, grab the vacuum and yes, you guessed it, the soft bristled attachment, and suck up the loose dust, hair, and fuzzies from the sill, sash, and panes. Go ahead, open the window, and suck up the dead bugs chilling between the window and the screen. Don't worry, dead bugs don't come back to life and crawl out of the vacuum, but empty the canister in case there were eggs. I prefer the crevice tool for this task, as it's not fun to pick dead bug bits from the bristles.

Now wash the glass itself. Large picture windows, those without separate panes, are most effectively cleaned with a squeegee and hot, barely soapy water. Use a soft rag or microfiber cloth to apply the water onto the glass and then remove with a squeegee.* If your home has many windows divided into small panes, it may be worth the time and effort to cut a squeegee to the width of the panes. Apply the soapy water to several panes, in the same row, squeegee, then wipe the frame. Work your way from top to bottom, left to right, naturally.

If you're lucky and have a newer home or newer windows, tilt-in sashes make window washing much easier than it used to be; but if not, even cleaning only the inside panes can make a significant difference. Windows with white sashes tend to collect dark-colored grime deep in the corners' crevices. As with white kitchen cabinets, if this bothers you, feel free to grab a few cotton swabs and the isopropyl (rubbing) alcohol. Remember, use a light touch with this technique, as it can remove some paint with the filth.

Walls

Are there pictures or mirrors that need dusting and cleaning? First remove any loose dust with a feather duster or the soft bristle attachment of your vacuum. Treat stained wood frames just as you do finished furniture, but never spray them with dusting spray. If you feel obligated to use dusting spray,** apply the spray to the cloth and then wipe. Otherwise, you'll create extra work when it comes time to clean the glass. Painted frames, whether wood, plastic, or metal, should be wiped with a damp rag. Finally, to clean the glass, spray glass cleaner onto a lint-free cloth or paper towel and wipe the glass. While glass and frames do a lot to protect photographs and documents from damage, they are not waterproof. Spraying glass cleaner onto the glass could allow liquid to seep into the frame and ruin your pictures or memorabilia.

* Quite possibly one of the most grin-inducing words in the English language. Say it, *squeegee*. See?
** Perhaps a relative is employed by a manufacturer of such a product.

Yes, I wish we were done with the walls, too, but it's time to check out the paint and switch plates. Doorframes are usually painted with a semigloss paint, and diluted white vinegar is amazing for removing smudges from doorframes and switch plates. Don't spray switch plates or electrical outlets with liquids—spray the cleaner onto the rag instead.

Dusting

It's time to dust. Contrary to popular belief, this is not the same as polishing. All surfaces, including furniture and electronics, need to be dusted; only wooden furniture should be polished. Be aware that many dusting sprays contain either wax or silicone.* If you choose to use a dusting spray, be aware that both of these ingredients build up over time, creating a film on wooden furniture. This film will have to be stripped away for the natural beauty of the wood to shine. For most painted wood, it's best to simply wipe the surface with a slightly damp rag. Do not confuse damp with dripping; wring the rag well before dusting. Just as we have approached cleaning in every room, work from top to bottom and left to right; not only does this method help you keep track of progress, it also continually pushes dust toward the floor, where it will eventually be swept or vacuumed away.

Electronics

Don't use dusting sprays on electronics or painted surfaces. Remember, liquid and electronics do not mix.** Microfiber cloths are excellent for cleaning computer monitors and television screens. If something sticky has

---

  * Yes, this is exactly how certain products can claim no-wax buildup.
 ** This is especially true when looking up old flames on the Internet.

Dusting Knickknacks

Dear Home-Ec 101,

My great-aunt Bertha* left me her Hummel collection. How on earth do I dust these items without losing my mind?

Signed,
Knickknack Patty Black

Oh, Patty I feel your pain. My father is a collector: plates, tiny houses, spoons. Basically, if it couldn't run away, you may find it in his home. I used to dread dusting those houses as part of my chores. I found using a clean, fan-style paintbrush worked well to whisk dust out of the trillions of crevices. That said, I hope ole Bertha also left you the curio cabinet. Keeping knickknacks displayed in a glass case helps reduce, but does not eliminate, the amount of dust they gather. Good luck and remember that just because someone else treasured an item does not mean you are obligated to do the same. Why do you think they invented eBay?

* Name changed to protect the guilty.

been splashed on a computer monitor or television screen, do *not* spray it with glass cleaner. The coating on a plasma television could be permanently damaged by the ammonia; just don't do it. Use a dry microfiber or lint-free cloth, such as an old T-shirt, to wipe away dust, and only wipe in straight lines. Never use a paper towel. There are ammonia-free solutions available, but distilled water works well, too. Dampen the cloth with the water and then wring it well before wiping the screen. Treat LCD computer monitors just as you would a plasma television.

Have you ever noticed how tangled cords draw dust bunnies like flies to honey? There is a reason for this phenomenon. The insulation, that's the plastic coating around the wires, has a static charge much like cling wrap in the kitchen. It's difficult to dust the rats' nest of wires often found behind our televisions and sound systems. A few dollar's worth of zip ties or Velcro strips can save a lot of headaches. Simply roll up the excess cord, much like you would a garden hose, and secure the coil with either a zip tie or a strip of Velcro. It's a simple fix, but it keeps things a lot neater. Just remember when you have to remove the zip ties to not accidentally snip the wire.

Furniture

Unlike mankind, not all wood furniture was created equal. Veneer, much like the dental appliance, is a plastic finish glued to another material, typically pressboard or wood pulp. Pressboard, or MDF, must be treated with care or it becomes disposable furniture, perfect for our disposable culture. If water comes into contact with the pulp beneath the veneer, the pulp swells and the laminate peels away. Sure, you can try to reglue it; you could also spend your time building a replica of the Taj Mahal from toothpicks and marshmallows. It can be done, but the end result may not be worth the effort. If the wood has warped, your best hope is to disguise the area until it can be replaced.

Wooden furniture must be polished to protect its finish.

Furniture made from actual wood, whether hard (oak) or soft (pine), can be finished with oil or varnish, which may show up in a variety of sheens (matte, low gloss, satin, or high gloss). When furniture is polished, it is actually the finish that you're buffing to a shine, and it is this layer that reduces moisture exchange between the wood and the atmosphere. If the

Recycled Dust Rags

Old T-shirts and cloth diapers work well for dusting and polishing as long as there are no buttons or zippers.

wood dries out too much, it may split, while if it absorbs too much moisture, it will swell. Polishing also helps fill in tiny cracks that would otherwise catch dust. When possible, follow the manufacturer's guidelines for care and maintenance. If the pieces have been purchased secondhand, this may not always be possible, but check the inside of drawers and the underside to see if there is a logo. Many companies post their care guidelines on the Internet, and they may be only a search away. Some websites suggest

Confession

I once tried cleaning a client's fake ivy in her white sink. The water suddenly turned green, as did her entire sink. I spent the rest of the session removing the dye from the disaster.

using cheap olive oil (pomace olive oil) instead of using commercial polish, but this really only pertains to oil-finished pieces, which is a common finish in some Scandinavian lines.

Whichever route you take, first wipe away any dust or grit to avoid marring the surface, then apply the polish with a soft cloth and buff away the excess. Polishing furniture does not need to be done frequently, unless you live in a very dry climate.

Older furniture may do well with paste wax. Apply this product generously in the direction of the grain of the wood. Always apply the entire length of the surface, or there will be stop and start marks. Allow the paste to dry for at least twenty minutes, but preferably several hours, then buff to a glossy shine, just as you would buff a car.

Fake Plants

When I cleaned houses for extra money, I developed an intense hatred of fake plants. I learned through trial and error that only plastic fake plants should be cleaned with water; silk plants are not always colorfast.

Dear Home-Ec 101,

Help! Our adorable, yet slightly dumb dog has decided to use the back of our lovely microfiber couch as a toilet! We contacted the manufacturer, who suggested spot cleaning the urine-stained area with diluted dish soap. This got the stains out. Unfortunately, the smell of pee still remains. I've (unsuccessfully) tried some pet cleaner and multiple soakings with an odor eliminator, but it just won't go away! Any suggestions?

Signed,
Noisome

First, check the care tag on your couch and make sure that it has a W or W/S on the tag (indicating that it is OK to clean it with a water-based cleaner). My guess is you did not immediately discover darling Fido had peed on the couch. If this is the case, urine probably soaked further into the couch than just blotting would fix. Use the upholstery attachment of a carpet cleaner to apply and remove a solution of equal parts water and white vinegar or an enzymatic cleaner. (Enzymatic cleaners are often found in both carpet care sections and pet sections of many big-box stores.) The goal is to make sure the cleaning solution penetrates as far as the urine. Yes, until the couch has thoroughly dried you will smell vinegar, but that odor dissipates quickly. When the couch is dry, the microfiber may feel a little stiff. Use a brush, like a nail brush, to gently brush the material until the fibers regain their normal texture.

Another possibility is that the urine dribbled down through a seam and soaked into the wood frame. I hope this is not the case, as it would be very difficult to remove without some disassembly. If you believe this to be the case, contact a professional through the helpline you first used to avoid voiding your warranty.

Silk plants should be dusted frequently. A feather or wool duster works well for this purpose as long as it is done often and the plant isn't too spiky. If it has been a while since you've paid these plants some attention, you'll find a somewhat sticky layer. Compressed air can blow away the filth, but this should be done outside. Plastic plants are a little more robust and can be cleaned by swishing in barely soapy water. Do not immerse the plant or get the moss, basket, or fake dirt wet, as these materials are usually quite flimsy and may not survive. Allow the plant to drip dry.*

Upholstered Furniture

Upholstered furniture should be vacuumed to remove hair, dirt, and crumbs according to the use it receives. A chair sitting undisturbed in a quiet room can get by with a seasonal vacuum, but a chair or couch in a busy family room with kids and pets should be vacuumed weekly. Dirt is the enemy; it filters down into the fibers creating extra friction, prematurely wearing the threads. Most upholstered furniture comes with a care tag that indicates what chemicals can or cannot be used to clean the fabrics:

- **W–W/S:** Clean with water-based cleaner.
- **S:** Spot clean with a solvent cleaner, such as isopropyl (rubbing) alcohol, no water.
- **WS:** Clean with foam from a water-based detergent.
- **X:** Dry clean only.

If your furniture is under warranty for stains, always consult with your manufacturer before attempting stain removal, as doing anything outside of their guidelines will void the warranty.

Leather furniture is usually quite durable, and with a little love it can outlast even families that seem determined to destroy it—go ahead, ask how I know. Leather furniture should be wiped down occasionally with a damp rag to remove dirt, hair, and dust. Once a season, these pieces should

---

* And wait for the captain to turn off the seat belt sign before returning to the upright position.

Missed a Spot?

Did you know that urine glows under a black light? If you're still having trouble with a urine smell after cleaning up a pet accident, borrow a black light from a friend.* When the room is as dark as possible (yes, by that I mean at night with all the lights off), turn on the black light and make sure your precious hasn't used any other areas of the couch or carpeting. Mark those areas with chalk. There are handheld black lights sold at pet stores for this purpose, if you can't borrow one.

* We all have a friend who never quite got over the sixties. For you youngsters, consider the quirky uncle who shows up in tie-dye.

be cleaned and conditioned with the leather cleaner and conditioner the manufacturer recommends. Do not use saddle soap on your furniture; this cleaner is far too harsh for most leathers designed for indoor use. Conditioning your furniture prevents cracking and helps keep the finish somewhat, but not perfectly, waterproof.

SEVEN

Bedroom Antics: Introducing Dust Mites; No One Sleeps Alone

If you exclude college, years spent couch surfing, and nights in the doghouse, most adults spend about one-third of their time in their bedrooms, which is reason enough to clean up a bit. Without delving too deeply into my past, I have seen bedrooms in worse condition than most, even if you're worried about a call from the health department.

Closets

Before getting started on this portion of the house, invest in adequate clothes hangers* and have three boxes or bins on hand. Label the containers something along the lines of *donate*, *trash*, and *repair*. If you are highly distracted, consider a fourth container for items that need to be put away in other rooms. Typically the approach to cleaning a room is top down and left to right, but this time there is a little organizing to do first.

Open the closet doors wide. Take a deep breath, and steady yourself on the doorjamb if necessary, because we are going in. First, locate the shelf

---

* Joan Crawford would disagree, but wire hangers are OK for a short time. Long-term use can damage clothing.

over the clothing bar. It may be cleverly disguised by years of neglect. Despite all appearances, there is a shelf under there. Beware of falling debris and begin unloading the shelf onto the bed (just tell Brian Wilson to move over). If you have a large walk-in closet, unload only one shelf at a time. One at a time, take a good look at each item and answer these questions:

1. Have I used this item within the last year?
2. Does this item have significant sentimental value? Do these memories make me happy? If not, is there a significant reason these memories should be revisited?
3. Is this item still useful for its intended purpose? Does it fit? Is it in style?
4. Am I realistic with my intention to save the item for future use?
5. If I give this item to a friend or relative, will the intended recipient keep the item only out of loyalty or guilt?
6. Is this item in blatant violation of local health ordinances?

Only return the items to the shelf if you can answer yes to at least one of the questions 1–4. If the answer is no, place the item either in the box labeled for donation or the disposal box. If you answer yes to question 5, the item is a good candidate for a charity donation. If you answer yes to question 6, I don't want to know.

Once the shelf has been cleared and sorted, it's time to locate the clothing bar. If you are unsure of whether or not to keep an item, turn the hanger backwards on the bar, so when you revisit this process in six months or a year, it'll be easy to tell which wardrobe items are seldom used.

Finding the Right Fit

When it comes to removing clothes from your closet, cut yourself significant slack if you are pregnant, have recently had a baby, or if the McRib has been brought back for a limited time. Don't torture yourself with pre-children clothing, but give yourself some time to settle into your new shape before starting from scratch.

If you hate an item of clothing, get rid of it. Unless you work for high-end fashion, the people who matter don't care if you show up in the same clothing frequently. All that really matters is that it is clean, fits, and is in good repair (see chapter 10 for preventing pesky wardrobe malfunctions). This process is somewhat time-consuming during the first cull, so be patient. Time spent sifting the wheat from the chaff will eliminate a lot of the "what should I wear?" morning waffle and reduce the amount of time you spend laundering items that were thrown on the floor for no reason.

Instead of simply arranging the shoes neatly, remove them from the closet and vacuum the flooring thoroughly. Break out the crevice tool and get into the corners and the no-man's-land that runs along the baseboard.

Shoes carry in a lot of debris, and this carpeting is some of the most neglected in a home. Place the shoes neatly in boxes or rows, putting any that need polishing or repairs in your repair bin.

Close the door tightly and be proud of what you've accomplished. You'll need this encouragement to get through the rest of the room.

Clutter Roundup

Place the bins in the hallway and gather up all lurking laundry, from the brassiere on the nightstand to the socks under the bed. Take these items to the hamper or laundry room. Dishes are next, yes even the water glass. Check under the bed for any food or dishes—don't act surprised, not only was I a teenager, I've had a million roommates and I've seen habits that

Shoe Storage

Store seasonal shoes somewhere other than on your closet floor. Late-night TV has plenty of examples of attractive under-the-bed storage units. Order now and receive a second one free!

How to Polish a Shoe

Save a trip to the airport: Polishing shoes is not a difficult chore. First, protect your work surface with newspaper or an old sheet. Clean patent leather shoes thoroughly with an old, damp rag. For best results, use a hair dryer to heat the shoe just before applying the polish. Be careful not to scorch the leather. Use the appropriate color of wax for the shoe and apply a good coat. Then moisten a corner of your polishing rag with water (spit optional) and buff to a gloss. This may require a little patience. Shoe polish prevents damage by keeping the leather supple and protecting it from the elements. Edge dressing is applied to the sides of the soles to cover scuffs.

would make Peg Bundy squirm. Next up, paper trash; scour the room and file or trash each piece as it is found. Phone numbers should be entered into your contact list* immediately and the scrap of paper discarded. Once all the clutter has been removed from the room, it's time to get down to actual cleaning.

Deep Cleaning

Up to this point, we've been organizing. Now we will get into the nitty-gritty of cleaning.

Dusting

Remove the comforter or bedspread from the bed; if it is time for it to be laundered, do so, otherwise simply set it out in the hall until the dusting is complete. It's easier to wash sheets than it is to clean a heavy bedspread or quilt.

---

* Little black books have been replaced by little BlackBerrys.

If your room has a ceiling fan, clean it as outlined in chapter 4. The dust bunnies (or buffaloes) will fall onto the bed or floor, where they can be disposed of properly. Grab your handy pillowcase-wrapped broom and inspect each corner where the ceiling and wall meet. Knock down any cobwebs. It doesn't matter whether the drapes or blinds are located in the bedroom or living areas, they are treated in the same manner discussed in chapter 6. It's also time to clean pictures and mirrors (again see chapter 6). Remember to never spray glass cleaner onto a picture frame—the liquid could seep into the frame and damage the contents. As we continue our top-down exploration of the bedroom, it is time to move onto the horizontal surfaces. That's right, work from left to right and clear the nightstand and dresser. If you or your partner has a tendency to unload the contents of your pockets onto the dresser, it may be wise to place a small basket or bowl as a catchall for these items. This keeps the entire surface from becoming the catchall. People are creatures of habit, so if a container has suddenly appeared, don't expect your partner to notice or even care right away.

Once the dresser and nightstand have been cleared, give each a thorough dusting and polishing.

The Bed

Moving lower, it's time to strip the bed and evict the dust mites. Every night we shed skin cells, which to a dust mite is like a $4.99 all-you-can-eat buffet. To this delightful mix add hair, oil, sweat, drool, and other bodily fluids

Confession

When I was a child and only had to worry about my room, I would tell my mother that the dust bunnies and I had signed a nonnegotiable peace treaty; I ignored them, they ignored me. I did not understand I was the unwilling participant in a lopsided arms race, my immune system versus their allergens.

Curing Musty Drawers

Dear Home-Ec 101,

An old roommate of mine borrowed a dresser from me and used it while we lived together. After she gave it back, the drawers had a musty smell that I couldn't get rid of. If I put any clothes in the drawers, they come out smelling funky and musty, too. What should I do?

Signed,

Funky in Fargo

Mold and mildew love nothing more than damp, still environments, which seems to be what your roommate created. Pull all of the drawers out of the dresser and give them a good wipe down with denatured alcohol. Typically one can find denatured alcohol at hardware stores, but I have also seen it at big-box stores. Thanks to the meth dealers, the quantity you can buy is limited and to avoid arousing government suspicions, I wouldn't purchase pseudoephedrine on the same shopping trip. Wipe all the interior surfaces with the alcohol to kill any mold or mildew spores. If the drawers are painted, a mild bleach solution may do the trick. The point of this exercise is to kill what is present before making the dresser less hospitable.

If you don't live in a swamp, set the drawers and dresser outside in the sun for a few hours to dry thoroughly. Otherwise, leave it disassembled in a dry room (not the basement) for a few days.

Give it a good sniff. Still funky?

Pick up cedar chips, the same kind used for pet bedding. Fill the drawers partway and shut them tightly. Again, give it a few days.

If your friend raised a powerful stink, you may have to resort to drastic measures. Yes, I'm afraid it's time to break out the sandpaper and lightly sand all of the interior surfaces. Try this method only if the drawers are solid wood. After sanding, apply a thin coat of varnish to all of the sanded surfaces to seal in any remaining odor.

and it quickly becomes apparent why there is more to this whole cleaning gig than simply straightening the covers and calling it a day. People with allergies should pay considerable attention to the materials in and around their beds, and those without allergies should pay attention in order to regale your friends and neighbors with riveting material at the next cocktail party.* Most of us spend a lot of time in bed or would like to, so it deserves some attention.

As with many household problems, prevention is key: Let your bed air out daily and no, I don't mean drag the whole thing outside. Just fold the sheets back toward the foot of your bed. Take a shower, eat breakfast, then make your bed. Dust mites love a moist environment; trapped moisture is the equivalent of rolling out the welcome mat. They'll hang out eating, breeding, and of course excreting. Yum.

Chances are mattresses are one of your larger household investments,** especially for someone just setting up his household. The lowly mattress pad isn't on the same domestic plane as a crocheted toilet-paper cozy, it's actually a quite functional household necessity. The mattress pad protects the mattress from body funk, spills, and stains. If soil and grime never actually reach the mattress, huzzah! People with allergies should opt to encase their pillows and mattress, especially if their bedding is several years old, in an allergen barrier. These tightly woven and zippered cases seal existing dust mites, their ancestors, and their crap where they can do no harm. A mattress pad should be washed every two weeks in hot water.

Change your sheets frequently—they are your mattress's first line of defense.*** Sheets and bedding other than down comforters should be washed in hot (at least 140°F [60°C]) water to kill dust mites.

---

  * Yes, I do spend a lot of time at home. Why do you ask?
 ** Eight thousand watts of high-def audio does not make up for the fact that you are sleeping in a dust mite burrito.
*** Technically a hot shower with soap is your mattress's first line of defense. Please, think of the mattress.

Caring for Bed Pillows

Dear Home-Ec 101,

I have two sons and a husband, and their pillows usually only last a year. I think they occasionally drool in their sleep, have sweaty heads, or explosive earwax. (My pillow is pristine, of course.) When the pillows get nasty, I just throw them out and buy new ones. It seems so wasteful! I hate spending money on new pillows. Is this what I'm supposed to do, or is there some secret method for washing pillows? Every time I've tried to wash one I've ended up with a sodden, lumpy mess that takes days to dry and never really re-forms into a pillow anyone is willing to use. I've tried using tennis balls in the dryer, but it has never worked for me.

Signed,

Fluffy

Pillows are veritable sponges for all the icky stuff that is part of being human. Prevention: To help keep pillows from becoming dirty in the first place, invest in zippered pillow protectors. There are ones specifically marketed as allergy barriers, and they can be a real blessing for those cursed with allergies. Additionally, changing pillowcases every few days will help prevent the pillow from absorbing oil and moisture. People with oily skin may find this helps with break-outs.

Washing: Always follow label directions, but typically, foam pillows should be washed by hand in the tub or a large sink with a mild detergent. Take care to rinse thoroughly and scrunch out as much water as possible before allowing to air dry. Down and synthetic-down pillows can be machine washed on the gentle cycle, but agitate them for only a minute or two, and add an extra rinse just to be on the safe side. As you have noticed, pillows typically are never quite the same after washing.

Calling it quits: Pillows should be replaced when they are lumpy, have to be fluffed for support, or when they no longer spring back after being folded in half. Typically this is somewhere between six months and two years depending on the quality. Old pillows make great pet bedding; give your local animal shelter a call to see if they can use some.

Spare Sheets

Each bed in a household should have two sets of sheets, minimum. Unless you are a chronic bed wetter with a bovine-sized bladder, you can store the second set of sheets flat between the mattress and box spring.

Individuals who are prone to acne should consider changing the pillowcase every or every other day.*

After the bed has been stripped, use the upholstery attachment to vacuum the mattress. This is the only cleaning technique that is recommended by several of the top-selling brands.

If your mattress is very stained and no longer covered by a warranty, consider having it steam cleaned by a carpet cleaning professional. If you opt to do it yourself, do not soak the mattress, and allow it to dry thoroughly before replacing the bedding. Mildew does not a fine bedfellow make; mattresses are not designed for their quick drying capabilities. If your mattress is dirtier than a vacuum can clean and still under warranty, contact the manufacturer for advice. Repeat after me: I will never use dry cleaning chemicals on a mattress. Not only can they damage the fibers, most are toxic.

If your bed is a coil spring mattress, it should be rotated 180 degrees seasonally and turned over every six months. Latex and memory foam mattresses should just be rotated. This simple, practically nonchore practice can extend the life and usability of your mattress by years.

---

* A lazy person may want to save time by layering a week's worth of pillowcases and removing one a day. Note: This does not work for underwear.

SECTION TWO

Wash It

EIGHT

Stains: Sure You Didn't Spill It

Life gets messy, and all too frequently some of the mess lands in your lap. Eating over your plate and using a napkin helps, but doesn't prevent all spills and stains. A clothes washer comes with multiple temperatures and settings for a reason, and it isn't just to confuse laundry n00bs.* Hot water is useful for getting out some stains, but it will damage some fabrics, and occasionally it is guilty of making some stains permanent. To effectively treat a stain, you need to know the type of stain (what caused it) and the type of fabric (check the label) you are dealing with.

The Basics

There are many variables when it comes to stain fighting, but one adage is always true: The sooner you address a stain, the greater the chance of saving the garment. However, it is important to note that some stains are forever. Some substances cause chemical reactions with the dye itself, and some chemicals, even those used to remove stains, can permanently damage

* If you're sheltered from web culture, n00b is an insult lobbed at inexperienced online gamers.

some fabrics. Always spot test any chemical or solution prior to treating a stain; do this on an inside seam.

Always rinse garments before moving from one stain treatment solution to another.

Stain sprays, sticks, and pens are most useful when used promptly. Always defer to label directions.

When a stain occurs, don't panic, and whatever you do, do not rub the mess into the fibers. When possible, work from the underside of the fabric, as this can help prevent the offending agent from being worked further into the fiber.

When attempting to remove a stain, remember the concept that like dissolves like. If the stain is caused by ink, remember that ink is a dye carried in a solvent. To remove the dye, before the solvent has evaporated, add more solvent to carry the dye back into solution. This is why so many people suggest spraying wet ink with hair spray. It's not that hair spray is a magic ink remover, it just has a high concentration of alcohol, which brings the ink out of the fibers and into solution.

After you dissolve the stain, it's time for some serious rinsing or wicking. Wicking is the process of a fiber absorbing a liquid. If you place a drop of water with food coloring on a paper towel, the drop will spread as it is absorbed by the fibers of the paper towel. A careful look would reveal that the dye does not spread as far as the water. The dye has larger molecules that don't move as easily.

Protect the Fabric

First determine what will remove the stain, then determine if it is safe for the fabric in question. Never use bleach on silk, wool, or spandex. Don't use acetone on acetate. Straight vinegar can weaken cotton, but if it's a choice between a ruined garment or weakened fibers, I know where I stand.

The goal when dealing with a stain is to cause the offending material to either wick into another fabric (usually a rag) or

The stain solutions in this chapter are given with the expectation that the instructions listed by the clothing manufacturer should be adhered to, or you risk voiding warranties or ruining the garment.

to be carried into the wash water, where it can be rinsed away. It is always useful to have a few cheap white cotton towels or rags around. The automotive section of many stores usually has white shop rags that are incredibly absorbent and make spot treating most stains a great deal easier.

Most stains fall into one of several general categories.

Protein

Many food items fall at least partly into this category, as will stains resulting from bodily fluids, wherever they originate. Proteins are organic compounds whose structure changes when heated, through a process called coagulation. When treating protein stains, it is important to keep the stain away from heat because heat could set the stain and make it permanent. Don't use hot water when treating this type of stain. New protein stains are significantly easier to treat than old, so if someone in the house has the stomach flu, it is better to at least soak the laundry casualties in cold water until the morning when they can be dealt with.

Immediately scrape away any solids, gently. Then soak the item in cold water with plain dish washing detergent—hand, not automatic. For small items use ½ teaspoon of detergent per quart of cold water. If you're bleary-eyed, in the middle of the night, this is just an estimate. In that case, get rid of the chunks, then toss the sheets into the tub with a dollop of dish detergent. Deal with it in the morning.

If it's not a crisis episode, let the item soak for at least fifteen minutes, swish it around and allow it to soak for at least another fifteen minutes.

Stain Care Triage

1. Don't panic, but take action as soon as possible!
2. Carefully remove any solid particles from the affected area without rubbing them in or spreading the offending matter.
3. Check the garment's label for the fabric type and specific care instructions.
4. Dissolve the stain following the principle that like dissolves like. Protein stains are best treated with cold water and agitation. Tannin stains are best treated with detergent, not soap (check the ingredient list on your laundry detergent to make sure). Oil stains are best treated with heavy-duty detergent and hot water. Grease stains are best treated with corn starch.
5. When the stain has dissolved, either rinse it or wick (blot) it away depending on the type of stain. Don't rinse stains that could spread, such as dyes.
6. Repeat treatment until the stain is gone, then launder as usual.

The swishing loosens any lingering stain, allowing the detergent to attack surfaces of the protein that were buried. Use either a commercial enzyme product, found in the laundry or pet aisle of most stores, or a liquid laundry detergent, and repeat the soak-swish method above. The two steps are especially important for older protein stains. If no stain is visible, rinse the item well, launder as usual, but be sure to check the site again before drying. Sometimes the staining agent gets deep into the fibers and just waits to reappear.

Protein stains: Antiperspirant, baby food, formula, blood, ring around the collar, dairy products, deodorant, egg white, feces, fish slime, gelatin, menstrual blood, mouthwash, semen, sherbet, urine, vomit, white glue.

Treatments for Common Stains

Stain	What to Use
Beer or Soda	Liquid detergent/white vinegar
Berry stains or grape juice	Liquid detergent/diluted ammonia (5%)
Blood (dried)	Liquid detergent/diluted ammonia (5%)
Butter, animal fat, or grease	Acetone
Chewing gum	Acetone
Chocolate	Liquid detergent/diluted ammonia (5%)
Coffee	Liquid detergent/white vinegar
Egg (raw) or milk	Liquid detergent in cold water
Grass	Pretreat with heavy-duty detergent, then bleach
Gravy	Liquid detergent in cold water
Grease (automotive)	Acetone
Ink	Acetone, then detergent (paint remover if all else fails)
Ketchup or mustard	Liquid detergent

Stain	What to Use
Latex paint (dried)	Paint remover, then detergent
Lipstick	Paint remover, then detergent
Mascara	Acetone, then detergent
Mildew	Diluted bleach (1 cup per gallon)
Nail polish	Acetone
Oil-based paint	Paint remover, then detergent
Pencil	Vacuum off bits, then detergent
Suntan lotion	Pine-based cleaner, then detergent
Tea (tannins) or tomato soup	Detergent
Tree sap	Turpentine, then detergent
Urine or vomit	Cold water, then white vinegar, then detergent
Wine	Liquid detergent (not soap)/diluted ammonia (5%)

Potty-Training Stains

Dear Home-Ec 101,

I am finally becoming successful in potty training my three-year-old, but he has a few accidents in his "big boy" underwear. I know to scrape as much of the mess as I can into the toilet, but beyond that, how do I launder it? I'm afraid bleaching would wipe the very important cartoon characters off of the underwear. Also, is there a way to wash the messy underwear with other clothes? I don't want to make an entire load of clothes icky, but I also don't want to waste the energy on washing just a few tiny clothing items alone. Thanks!

Signed,

Grossed Out Greta

When your son has an accident, instead of just scraping off what you can, give the underwear a good swish in the toilet. Flush first! Your goal is to rinse it out as much as humanly possible. Unless the potty trainee has been marinating in his accident for a while, this will remove all but trace amounts of fecal matter.

Bleach is safe for colorfast prints, and when you use it in the amount needed for disinfecting, you don't have to worry about the tyke's favorite characters. You only need 1 tablespoon of chlorine bleach per gallon of water. Wash the underwear with hot water, detergent, and bleach in the bathroom sink; rinse it well and hang it to dry so it doesn't mildew. Toss it in the next full load and carry on with life.

Oxygen bleach (a.k.a. sodium percarbonate, a.k.a. OxiClean and other brands) is also an alternative worth considering when the laundry needs a germ-fighting boost. Sunlight and the dryer both work well to kill any lingering germs.

Don't overload your clothes washer. To keep soil and germs from being deposited on clothing, the washer must be able to adequately rinse the dirt away. This is especially true for high-efficiency models that use significantly less water.

Please don't forget to clean the sink and thoroughly wash your hands, paying attention to your fingernails. Kids are germ factories and you don't want to be a vector (that's the person who infects others a la Typhoid Mary).

Tannin Stains

Tannins are natural compounds found in plants and in many foods and drinks made from plants. These compounds are what give wine that puckery, dry feeling when sipped. They react with some alkaline chemicals, which is why using soap on a tannin stain can make it permanent. When dealing with a liquid spill, it is safest to treat it as a tannin stain unless you are sure of its origin.

Tannin stains: Coffee, fruit drinks and juices, ketchup, mustard, soft drinks, tea, wine

For all washable fabrics, try the following method: With any solids (such as mustard and ketchup) gently scrape off any excess. Rinse under cool running water. If the stain is still present, work from the wrong side of the garment. Place a white towel or rag underneath to create a stain-absorbing pad. In a spray bottle, mix equal parts water and vinegar or lemon juice with a tiny amount of liquid laundry detergent (about 1 teaspoon per cup of solution). Spray the affected area and blot on the towel until gone. Rinse with plain water to stop the acid from weakening the fibers, then launder as usual.

Dye Stains

Because dye is designed to leave a color behind, once it has dried, there is a high probability that this stain is permanent. With washable fabrics, first try using a high pH to bring the stain into solution. Soak the freshly stained garment for fifteen minutes in a solution of 1 quart of warm water, ½ teaspoon liquid laundry detergent, and 1 tablespoon ammonia. Then rinse the item. For the second step, try an acidic version of the soak: 1 quart warm water and 1 tablespoon vinegar. If the stain is dry or set when it is found, try

Dye stains: Food coloring, grass stains, hair dye, ink, markers

Mildew Stains

Dear Home-Ec 101,

I've just discovered that my built-in wardrobe became damp and mildewed over winter. While most of my clothes have survived, my beautiful blue satin evening gown was closest to the wet spot. Despite being stored in a dress cover, it has mildew stains and watermarks all over it. I'm happy to risk washing it, either by hand or the gentlest machine setting (I machine washed my vintage wedding dress on the advice of a vintage clothing specialist), but I don't know what sort of detergent to use.

Signed,
Mildewed Mel

Mildew is a living organism that chows down on natural fibers such as cotton or linen. Satin is actually a term that describes the weave of the fabric, not the actual fibers. Your success depends on how long the mildew has had to penetrate the fibers; it is possible your dress has been ruined. Before going the oxygen-bleach route, try applying a paste of borax and water on the spots unless there are a lot; in that case, soak the entire dress in a solution of 1 cup borax per quart of water. This is pretty heavy-duty, so proceed with caution. Rinse the dress well before line drying. If that doesn't work, try the oxygen bleach (a.k.a., sodium percarbonate) route. With either solution, it is imperative to test on an inside seam before dunking the entire dress. As a last resort, try lemon juice and salt on the stains and let the material dry in the sun. This would be a first choice for white cotton fabrics, but in your case, you want to preserve the color of the material. The lemon and salt solution may cause the fabric to bleach; it depends on the dye used by the manufacturer.

dabbing the stain with isopropyl (rubbing) alcohol. Work from the wrong side of the garment over an absorbent pad—that trusty white cotton towel. Move the absorbent pad frequently as more alcohol is applied.

Grease Stains

Treat a stain as oil-based when it is from a simple source such as the oil from a car or the spatter from frying bacon. Use the dull side of a knife to gently scrape away any grease that has not been absorbed by the fiber. Generously sprinkle both sides of the fabric with cornstarch or talcum powder and gently press the powder into the stain. Allow the powder to sit for at least thirty minutes, then shake or brush away the

Grease stains: Automotive grease, oil, baby oil, bacon grease, cooking grease/oil, petroleum jelly

residue. This process can be repeated several times using fresh cornstarch. If some stain persists, rub liquid laundry detergent into the stained area and allow it to sit before laundering the garment in the hottest water safe for the fabric. When oily stains are caused by other food items, such as mayonnaise or salad dressing, try to remove as much of the oil as possible before treating the protein portion, but do not apply heat until the protein portion of the stain has been removed.

The same goes for cosmetic items such as lipstick and foundation: Treat the oil-grease portion of the stain before attempting to remove the dye.

NINE

Odors: Rolling Down the Window Is Not Always an Option

The best way to fix laundry odors is to keep them from happening in the first place. While regular dirty laundry is no bouquet of roses, laundry that has mildewed absolutely reeks (and it's a deep reek that won't come out easily.) For mildew, nothing signals "welcome, come on in, make yourselves at home" more than a warm, moist environment—like the one found in a pile of laundry.

Was That You, or the Washing Machine?

Sometimes it's not even the laundry itself that has the mildew problem. Clothes washers can be the source of many laundry room odors. Once a month, run an empty load of hot wash, cold rinse and add chlorine bleach. This will kill off any mildew in the machine.

Both mineral and detergent buildup also provide a nice home for stinky mildew. If you have hard water, alternate the bleach cycle with a vinegar cycle on a month-by-month basis to remove hard water and detergent buildup from inside the washtub. Do not combine chlorine bleach and vinegar in the same cycle. Using the right amount of laundry detergent goes a long way

Musty Jeans

Dear Home-Ec 101,

For a few weeks, I've occasionally noticed a musty smell. At first I thought it was something in my house, but I couldn't pin it down. I finally realized it was my favorite pair of jeans! I think they sat too long in the washer, but I've washed them several times since, and they still smell. I'm not ready to part with these pants.

Signed,
Little Suzy Stinky Pants

It sounds like you have a case of detergent buildup. This sticky residue can trap all kinds of funky odors. This usually happens with heavier fabrics and more commonly in high-efficiency washers. The easiest solution is prevention. Always use the least amount of laundry soap possible to effectively clean the clothes and add vinegar to the final rinse.

In your case, it's a little too late for prevention. If you have a programmable washer, use hot water, place vinegar in the prewash dispenser, borax powder in the main wash, and add an extra rinse. If you have a standard washer, run with vinegar in the wash water, rinse, then use borax in the next wash cycle, and finish with a plain water rinse.

Dry your jeans thoroughly, and you should be stink-free!

toward preventing odor issues. Too much laundry detergent may result in the rinse cycle not flushing away all of the detergent. A sticky residue is left on clothing, which causes items to become veritable dirt and odor magnets. Always use the proper amount of detergent when washing clothing. Consider adding vinegar to the rinse cycle in place of fabric softener. Use ¼ cup for front-loading washers and ½ cup for top-loading washers. This frugal tactic improves the effectiveness of the rinse cycle and can help prevent detergent buildup.

High-efficiency washers have tight seals to prevent water leaking during operation;

Mildew is just the common name for various molds that live and grow in damp, still environments.

the drawback to these seals is that they also prevent air circulation, which means the washtub may not dry properly and mildew may start growing. If you have a high-efficiency washer, wipe the seal and leave the door open when the machine is not in use so it can dry thoroughly. Pet owners and parents should always check the machine before adding laundry. Fluffy won't be too happy about a ride on spin cycle.

Wet Laundry

Towels and washcloths are some of the biggest offenders and are often the source of moisture for mildew growth. Never throw wet towels into a hamper. After bathing or swimming, hang damp or wet towels on a towel hook, a bar, the back of a chair, or even over a door; the possibilities abound. Washcloths should be wrung out after use and hung to dry. While it's true, they don't make the most attractive design elements, most people are just happy to discover someone practices good hygiene.

Dry wet clothing as soon as possible. Try not to let clean items sit in a closed washer for an extended length of time. In some humid areas of the country, clothing can begin to mildew in less than a day. If you are prone to forgetting about clothing in the washer, try setting a timer as soon as you place a load in the appliance.

The Down Low on B.O.

Body odor is a big problem for many people, and some of the blame falls at the feet of salts from perspiration. When people sweat, it isn't just water,

Dear Home-Ec 101,

In the course of my "Grand Poo-bah of the Home" duties, I forgot about a load of wash in the washing machine. Of course, it's almost the entire wardrobe for both my children, and the entire load reeks of mildew. I've rewashed the load at least three times now using a total of two gallons of white vinegar, but the offensive odor remains. Yipes!

Signed,
What's a Poo-bah to do?!

The next step would be to soak the clothing in a borax solution of 1 cup borax to 1 quart water. Be sure to test the fabric for colorfastness before soaking. Rinse the clothing thoroughly and allow the garments to line dry in direct sunlight.

Unfortunately, these second-tier methods for removing mildew are a little harsh and may cause some premature wear on the fabric. However, it is better than relegating the items to the trash.

there are salts, too. When the sweat evaporates, these salts are left behind. These salts are what cause pit stains on your favorite white T-shirt. Sweat stains are best treated immediately. While still damp, the sweat is acidic and is best treated with a weak base, such as baking soda. Dissolve baking soda in water and spray or sponge onto the affected area. Allow the garment to sit for approximately half an hour. Launder in cold water (heat may set any lingering perspiration stains, making them difficult, if not impossible, to remove). Baking soda is an excellent tool for combating odor problems; repeat the process if necessary.

Older stains require an acid; diluted vinegar sprayed or sponged onto the offending area will help remove the stain and kill off any offending

Chemical Smells On New Clothes

Dear Home-Ec 101,

Could you please tell me what that awful chemical smell is on some new jeans? How can I get rid of it? I tried adding 1 cup of vinegar in my wash with soap three times, and they still stink. I really love the jeans and hope you have a solution for me.

Signed,

Chemical Clara

The smell you are referring to is most likely formaldehyde. In clothing manufacturing formaldehyde is used because, in theory, when combined with urea (Yes! That's pee! Ewwww!), it makes the clothing more wrinkle resistant, stain resistant, and is a disinfectant. (What self-respecting germ could survive that?)

So, what's the best way to get rid of the smell? Borax and/or baking soda.

In your case, I'd probably use a cup of baking soda or borax per load of new clothing. It may take several washings, as some companies are now using even stronger disinfectants and even pesticides to protect the clothing during shipment and storage.

odors. Allow the solution to sit for thirty minutes. Again, launder in cold water to avoid setting the stain. Repeat as necessary.

Sunlight is great for whitening fabrics; drying a fabric in the sun may help lighten any faint stains.

For a stubborn perspiration stain or for treating an unwashable garment, make a paste of 1 tablespoon cream of tartar and three crushed full-strength aspirin tablets—for Pete's sake, make sure they are the uncoated white variety—mix with a little water and gently apply to the area with an old toothbrush. Rinse with plain water and air dry.

Other Offending Odors

Urine. Pee stinks. Whether it's a child or a pet that had the accident, sometimes the odors left behind can be foul. For the best odor removal, use an enzymatic cleaner (found in the laundry or pet section of big-box stores) to help clear up any lingering odor.

Down. Some items, such as down comforters and pillows, stink simply because they are wet. If you have washed a down comforter or pillow, it can take several cycles in the dryer (with a couple of tennis balls for good measure) to completely dry. Once the down is dry, the odor will be gone, too.

Grease. Kitchen grease is a common source of funky odors in laundry. Keep kitchen towels, washcloths, and aprons isolated from the rest of the laundry, and wash these items in the hottest water possible with sufficient detergent and an ample rinse cycle to ensure the soap has been rinsed away. Smell the wash load; if there is a lingering odor of grease, a trip through the dryer is not going to improve the situation. A second wash may be required. As a veteran of commercial kitchens, I found Simple Green to be an effective laundry additive that can help with eau de kitchen funk; it helps dissolve the grease so it can be flushed away rather than deposited on clothing. As always, test the cleaner on an inconspicuous area on the garment.

TEN

Minor Garment Repair: Beyond Dental Floss and Staples

Not knowing how to sew isn't an excuse for wearing ill-fitting clothes that are in disrepair. You can plead poor taste and bad fashion, maybe, but not ignorance. Most garments have a few warning signs before failure. As a clothing item ages, the materials used to construct the piece weaken; this natural process can be accelerated by using water that is too hot for the material, using harsh detergents, or by insisting pants still fit. In all of these cases, sooner or later something will give, and Murphy's Law will surely be the rule of the day.

While taking care of your laundry, check the clothing for items that need repair. As each piece is folded or hung, give the seams and fasteners a quick once-over. Loose threads are often a signal that a closer look is needed. If an important event, such as an interview, is on the horizon, check the

Confession

I've used mint waxed dental floss to fix a button. I had a needle, but couldn't be bothered to pick up any thread.

garment at least the night before. Emergency sewing kits are inexpensive and you should own several for easy access. Keep one in a purse or brief-case, another in your glove compartment, and one in your home, preferably in a place you will remember.

Following are some quick fixes for common wardrobe malfunctions.

Missing Drawstrings

Sweatpants and hooded sweatshirts have drawstrings that can be destroyed by the dryer or an annoying child. To repair the beloved item, untangle the drawstring or find a similar cord of the same length and thickness as the original. Poke the sharp end of a large safety pin through the cord or ribbon. Close the safety pin and insert it into one of the two original open-ings (these should be checked for fraying; if necessary they can be repaired in the same manner as a buttonhole). The safety pin allows the cord to be worked through the hood or seam. Thread the cord all the way through, then remove the safety pin.

Zippers

Zippers can be as difficult as they are useful. A stuck zipper is frequently caused by the slider accidentally grabbing material and zipping it into the teeth. If your zipper is stuck, stop tugging on the zipper immediately and examine both sides to locate the pinched material. Gently pull out as much of the fabric from the teeth as possible, then unzip the zipper.

If the teeth of the zipper are catching on one another due to age, run the tip of a pencil* along the teeth. The graphite will act as a lubricant, without pesky grease stains.

A safety pin can hold a separated zipper together, but it's not a perma-nent solution. If the teeth no longer align, grab a pair of needle-nose pliers and open the band at the base of the zipper. Once the bottom is open, both

* No. 2, always no. 2.

sides of the zipper can move freely; move the slider to the bottom and realign the teeth. Zip partway and either bend the band back into place or thread a needle with a strong piece of thread and stitch tightly around the base of the zipper itself. Use the thread to re-create a version of the band that was removed.

Hemlines

A hippie hem is always an option, but it doesn't do much for one's professional appeal. Unless you're experienced in working with denim, jeans should be taken to a tailor. A simple hem job is usually inexpensive; just bring your inseam measurement. It's easiest to obtain your inseam measurement by using a pair of pants that fit well. Lay the pants flat on the floor and measure the length of the seam from the crotch along the inside of the leg to the bottom of material. Ladies, remember to account for the length of the heel that will be worn with the pants to be altered.

Changing a Hemline

Most pants that are not jeans are simple to hem. It is best to let out a hem as soon as possible after purchase before a permanent blemish due to wear appears at the original length. In addition to matching thread and a needle, straight pins, a seam ripper, and an iron are useful. Use the seam ripper to carefully cut the thread of the old hem, be careful not to damage the fabric of the garment. Use your iron to press out the old seam. Pin the pants at the desired length and use the iron to press the new seam. Use a basic, straight stitch about ½ to 1 inch from the bottom of the pants. If the pant leg was shortened by a large amount, for an adult, it may be necessary to cut some of the excess fabric to prevent the hang of the pant from being altered by bulk.

Temporary Hemline Fix

Dear Home-Ec 101,

The hem is pulling out of my neutral fall-back pants, the ones I wear nearly every day when I'm not inspired to pick out anything else. The stylishness and variety of my wardrobe aside, there is no way I'm actually fixing that sucker with a needle and thread right now—when I sew on buttons, they last for about a week. Can you suggest any short-term fixes until I can get someone else to properly repair them?

Signed,

Hemingway I'm Not

If you are truly against sewing or simply need a way to make it through the day without your hem completely falling out, here are a few quick fixes.

__Tape:__ this works best if the pants aren't cuffed. Scotch tape may be clear, but it's not invisible.

__Safety pins:__ Do not be afraid to use more than one.

__Fusible webbing or hem tape:__ If your pants can take the heat of an iron, consider this no-sew, but more durable solution. These items are readily available at sewing and craft stores.

Replacing Buttons

Replacing a button is simple. Thread a needle with a 12-inch (30cm) piece of string, move the needle to the center of the string, and tie the two loose ends together with a knot. Start from the wrong side of the fabric and poke the needle through the desired location. Ideally the needle should also go through one of the holes in the button. If the button has two holes, return the needle to the back side of the fabric through the second hole. If there are four holes and the garment has more than one button, match the pattern of the stitch to the other buttons. Sometimes the buttons are sewn using an X pattern, while other manufacturers use parallel lines. When the button is secure, sew two or three additional stitches, but do not pull the thread taut. On the back side of the fabric, secure the thread by running the needle under the loose stitches and tying a knot. Snip the thread close to the new knot to release the needle.

Frayed Buttonholes

If the stitching around a buttonhole comes loose, the button will have a tendency to slip from the hole. Reinforcing the hole will keep the button in place. Don't get overzealous or the button will no longer fit.

A buttonhole stitch is very similar to a blanket stitch, which is used to finish the raw edge of—wait for it—blankets. Thread a needle with a 12- to 18-inch (30cm to 46cm) piece of thread, center the needle on the string, and tie the two loose ends together in a knot and begin on the wrong side of the fabric, poke the needle through the fabric approximately an ⅛-inch (3mm) from the opening of the buttonhole, tuck the tail of the knot between the layers of the material, if possible. Return the needle to the wrong side of the fabric by passing it through the buttonhole and not through the material itself, but do not pull the thread tight; leave a loop. Poke the needle back through the fabric next to the 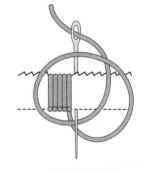 first point, but this time when returning the needle through the buttonhole, also pass the needle through the loop of thread from the first pass. Pull the first stitch tight. Repeat this all the way around the buttonhole, then on the wrong side of the fabric, pass the needle through several stitches, tie a knot, and snip the thread, close to the knot.

Hire Out

If there are clothing repairs to be made, but no initiative in the sewing department, take heart. Simple repairs can be trusted to almost any dry cleaner. However, more complicated tasks, such as altering a suit jacket, should be made in a less haphazard fashion than simple proximity. The best recommendations are word of mouth, but sometimes those in the know don't run in your circle. This is an instance where flattery may get what you need. Compliment a well-dressed acquaintance and ask for the name and number of her tailor. Most people respond positively to flattery and are happy to give a referral.

ELEVEN

Laundry: The World's Most Thankless Chore

Everyone has laundry, even nudists. They still have towels, sheets, and hopefully aprons. Can you say grease splatter?

It has been said that the invention of the modern washing machine has been one of the greatest laborsaving devices introduced to the home. What was once a sweaty, backbreaking chore now takes only a fraction of the effort. Modern homes have hot water available at the touch of a button, and still people complain about having to carry clothing up and down an entire set of stairs. Oh, the humanity of it all.

Clothes washers use three methods to clean soiled laundry: thermal energy (heat), physical energy (the swishing or tumbling), and chemical energy (hello, detergents). The sturdier the fabric, the more it tolerates each of these methods. Delicate fabrics are best cleaned by laundry detergent because the fibers can be weakened or damaged by friction or heat. Laundry detergent surrounds dirt and grease, and suspends them in the water, allowing them to be rinsed away. The detergent's ability to surround the dirt and grease is what keeps the dirt from simply redepositing on all of the clothing in the water.

Dingy Laundry Worries

Dull, dingy, or generally gray laundry is often a symptom of too much or too little detergent. If you live in an area with hard water, it may be necessary to use more than the manufacturer's recommendation because some of the detergent gets used up on the minerals in the water instead of on the dirt on the clothes. Try adding a little more to your next wash, or add a nonprecipitating water conditioner to the washer. (Nonprecipitating will keep the minerals that make the water hard from depositing on the fabric.) If you're heavy-handed with the detergent, try rewashing clothing in the hottest water safe for the garments, with only a water conditioner and no additional detergent; follow with a cool rinse.

Laundry Is a Team Event

In most cases, if more than one person is creating the mess, more than one person can address the situation. Even toddlers can help sort clothing before it is washed, and as soon as children are old enough to pull their dresser drawers open, they should be asked to assist with putting away their clothing.

Individuals and couples can usually get away with running only a load here or there. Once a child enters the picture, the scale of laundry commitment increases exponentially, and that doesn't even take into consideration those who opt to cloth diaper. Sure, their clothing is tiny, but as luck would have it, they tend to be unable to control their bodily fluids. By the time good hygiene is grasped, their clothing is big enough to make an impact.

Busy families may find a load-a-day approach works well; yes, even in dual-income families. Start a load of laundry while the coffee drips its magic, and it should be done before the last person leaves the house in the morning. The first person home in the afternoon or evening can shuffle the

Washing Instructions for Various Fabrics

Material	Washing Method	Special Instructions
Acetate	Dry clean or handwash	Some solvents, such as acetone, will destroy this fabric.
Acrylic	Warm wash	Some items are not suitable for the dryer (many knits).
Cotton	Warm or hot wash	Cotton tends to wrinkle; don't over dry.
Linen	Refer to the label; most garments and household linens are washable.	Napkins, sheets, and apparel become softer with frequent washing. Hang white linens in the sun to whiten.
Microfibers	Usually machine washable	Susceptible to heat damage and static.
Nylon	Warm wash	

laundry into the dryer. In families, folding and putting away is a good community; activity delegate as appropriate.

While I'm all about relaxing when possible, I'm not sure that grabbing the last pair of underwear should be a reminder to actually start doing laundry. Don't waste time feeling self-conscious if the dirty laundry has

Material	Washing Method	Special Instructions
Olefin/ Polyolefin	Cold wash	Very susceptible to heat damage, but highly stain resistant
Polyester	Machine safe	Dry on low; hang or fold promptly.
Rayon	Some garments are hand washable, but defer to the label instructions.	Rayon is very susceptible to stretching when wet. Use care.
Silk	Dry clean (usually)	Pre-washed silk is hand washable with mild soap. Never use chlorine bleach on silk. Lay flat or hang dry.
Spandex	Machine wash, warm or cold	Drip dry and never use chlorine bleach.
Wool	Dry clean	Let wool rest/air out between wearings to regain its shape and prevent the need for excess cleaning.

been piling up; it has happened to everyone. Sometimes the pile of laundry is triggered by sickness, coming home from a vacation, or just getting behind. If a more laid-back approach to laundry maintenance has been adopted, perhaps the marathon method is an appropriate remedy.

Dear Home-Ec 101,

I have what is probably a stupid question, but I'd really love an answer. If I have a particularly dirty load of laundry, (say, we woke up to find the cat had puked on the bed), does it do any good to add extra laundry detergent? In other words, does more detergent equal cleaner laundry?

Signed,
Kickin' the Cat

Actually, no, more detergent is not better and your clothes may actually attract more dirt with excess detergent because a dirt-attracting residue may be left on your clothing. If you have something that is especially dirty and want it cleaner, pretreat it with a stain remover, and then wash it in a smaller load than usual, but use the same setting on the washer. (For example, if you usually wash on the large setting, then keep it set to large, but wash a small-sized load.) The additional water flowing through your clothes will help in getting the item cleaner.

And why is it that cats always puke on the bed?

Know Your Weapons

Detergent

Laundry detergent comes in two basic forms, liquid and powder. The liquid form can do double duty as a pretreatment for stains. Typically, liquid detergents are better at getting out grease and food-based stains. Powdered detergents are slightly better at removing ground-in dirt and may be a good choice for outdoors people.

Some people are sensitive to perfumes and dyes. Thankfully, most detergents are now available in perfume- and dye-free formulas. Clean clothes don't need perfumes to smell fresh.

Laundering Lingerie

Despite what an extremely popular women's lingerie store insists, most brassieres can be washed on the delicate cycle of newer washing machines. Just be sure they can't get tangled up with other clothing. By all means, if the washer is a hand-me-down dinosaur, hand wash your lingerie in the sink.

Use care when using ultraconcentrated forms of detergent. Follow the manufacturer's directions. It typically contains less water or filler, and the average load will need less than the nonconcentrated versions.

Bleaches

Chlorine and nonchlorine bleaches both help remove stains and brighten whites. Chlorine bleach, or sodium hypochlorite, is stronger, but not safe for all fabrics and colors; keep it away from silk and wool. Always test it in an inconspicuous location, as directed on the label.

Add chlorine bleach five minutes after the wash cycle has started. Sodium hypochlorite can destroy the enzymes in some detergents, so give them a chance to work first.

Chlorine bleach has the added benefit of being a disinfecting agent, useful in other areas of the home. Nonchlorine bleach is safe for colors but is less effective at brightening whites. It is also more effective in warm water than cold.

Pretreating Stains

Stain pretreaters show up as sprays, sticks, gels, and pens. The liquid type should be applied to stains a few moments before launder-

The sooner a stain is treated, the better your chances are of removal.

ing so it can be washed out immediately, but the stick form can be applied any time, even days in advance of washing, without harming the garment. Remember to test first.

Sort

First separate the clothing by color; start simply with the good old whites, lights, and darks. Then separate by fuzz creators versus fuzz collectors; for instance, keep the towels and fleece away from the blankets and corduroy. The fuzz creators shed their lint in the wash, while the collectors happily grab it and hang on tight. Next up, separate the natural fibers from synthetic fibers. They don't dry at the same rate, so separating them is a simple energy-saving trick if you already have two loads. Lastly, separate delicate items from heavy, durable ones. Don't break out the scale, it's not that particular, just keep silks and rayons out of the denim pile. Once the items have been sorted, break any extra-large piles into load-size piles.

While sorting, empty pockets, turn jeans inside out, fasten bra hooks, and place delicate items in a mesh laundry bag. Then pretreat stains (see chapter 8 for stain advice).

Sorting Stripes

When in doubt with striped items, wash in cold with the darker of the two colors.

Start the First Load

Select the appropriate size and wash temperature for your load. If it's a particularly dirty load of light-colored cottons, hot water is fine. For most other fabrics and dyes, warm and cold water is best. Always use a cold-rinse—doing otherwise is simply a waste of energy. Allow extra-dirty clothes more room to move in the machine by washing smaller loads.

Set a Timer Within Earshot
It's easy to forget a load and unintentionally extend the chore, or to forget about a load entirely and later discover it rank and mildewed. Some newer clothes washers are equipped with end-of-cycle signals; pure brilliance.

Pick Your Folding Battles

Folding laundry takes enough time, so why fold underwear? Think hard, when was the last time you saw wrinkly underwear? If you're in an auto accident and they have to strip all your clothes off, do you think the paramedics are going to laugh at your wrinkly underwear? No, of course not, they'll be too busy laughing at your holey underwear. Take away: Throw out the holey underwear and don't bother folding the ones you keep.

Empty the Dryer Promptly

Transfer clothing from the washer to the dryer. If you have a large-capacity washer, it may be necessary to divide the load for drying. Shake larger items before tossing them in the dryer; balled-up clothing dries slowly and creates wrinkles.

Set the dryer on low for: Acrylic, nylon, polyester, polyolefin, and microfibers. Remember not to overdry clothing, as this can set wrinkles and shrink some fabrics such as cotton. Fold, hang, and store items promptly.

Navigating the Laundromat

Sometimes even a marathon laundry day is not enough to play catch-up. These situations are often caused by stomach viruses, notes from the school nurse with strict instructions on how to rid a home of head lice, a broken washer, or avoidance due to depression. Whatever the cause, a true

Durable Denim

Jeans, especially dark washes, should be laundered inside out; this prevents fading due to friction.

mountain of laundry may warrant a trip to the Laundromat to reset the routine. If possible, bring a friend; if not, a book. Aside from people watching, Laundromats aren't exactly known for their high entertainment value. Remember, there are some items that shouldn't ever be taken to a Laundromat. The rule of thumb is, if you can't live without an item, hand wash it at home.

If it would break your heart to lose your favorite shirt, hand wash it in the sink instead of taking it to the Laundromat.

Here are some tips that will make your Laundromat experience more palatable:

- Assemble all laundry paraphernalia into one basket or bag. Dorm-style shower caddies make fantastic laundry supply carriers.
- Presort the laundry, and pretreat the stains before leaving home. Pillowcases make excellent laundry bags, but don't be ashamed to cart the clothing in trash bags if there aren't enough pillowcases. There is no such thing as haute couture at the Laundromat.
- Get change before going. Most Laundromats have a change machine or surly attendant, but sometimes they are out of order or out of quarters.
- Before adding clothing, always check the washer for strays from the last customer—a lone red sock can do an incredible amount of damage.
- Always sniff the bleach dispenser to ensure dark clothing won't be speckled with someone's leftover bleach. If the odor of bleach is present, run a load of whites in that machine.

Reader Confession

Never let your sorority sisters talk you into going out for, ahem, just one beer while waiting for clothing to dry. Folding with a hangover is awful. —Anonymous

Respect Common Laundry Space

If your apartment building has a communal laundry room, always be courteous when using it. Set a timer in your unit to avoid hogging a machine. Leave a labeled basket by the washer or dryer just in case the clothing is left unattended for an extended period of time. Consider leaving a note with a contact number so your neighbor has an opportunity to avoid touching your soggy knickers.

- Bring paper towels, a few rags, or even used dryer sheets to wipe out the inside of the dryers before loading with clean clothes. The only thing worse than finding hair, human or otherwise, on clean clothing is finding someone else's hair.
- Always check the dryer before adding clean items, and empty the lint trap. If it is at all feasible, consider line drying all but the sturdiest items at home; dryers seem to be the source of much of the clothing damage that can occur: rust spots, burn marks, etc.

How Does One Avoid Creating a Mountain of Laundry?

If a washer and dyer is available, start by not procrastinating. Just like doing dishes, some chores are just easier without the additional pressure of being behind. Try to make folding and putting laundry away as much of a habit as possible. Folding a single dryer load is annoying enough; facing a mountain of clean clothes is downright disheartening. Here are some quick tips to keep the piles from multiplying.

- Keep the laundry room clean. Just like a clean sink can inspire one to actually place a dish in the dishwasher, a clean laundry room has the potential to inspire someone to begin a load without coercion. Maybe.
- Limit the amount and type of clothing owned. The fewer clothes a person owns, the more often laundry chores must be performed

Reduce the Laundry Piles

If a young child has a habit of pawing through her dresser and dropping rejected wardrobe options onto the floor, take the time to oversee the reversal of that process. Yes, it's a pain, and of course you don't have time for it, but long term, it will significantly reduce the amount of needless laundering. Proactive parenting, the green choice. Who knew?

before hygiene standards nosedive. This is especially true with young children. Without counting school uniforms, understand that it's perfectly acceptable for a kid to wear the same outfit every few days. In fact, most young children even like routine and have a few favorite items. With rare exception, no one needs more than a week plus a day's worth of underwear. Ladies, I'm not talking about the few less-than-perfect pairs we keep for those days—just hang on to those.

- Save time sorting socks; straight out of the dryer, white athletic socks can appear quite similar. Use a fabric marker and put an identifying mark under the toe of each sock to establish ownership. It's easy for anyone to match a symbol or number of dots instead of looking for subtle differences in size or texture.

- Store off-season clothing. Sure, the dresser or closet may be large enough to hold the items, but if children are around, there is always the possibility of washing sweatshirts even when the temperature has been in the triple digits for over a week.

- Sometimes items such as jeans, pants, skirts, and dresses can and should be worn more than once. Don't throw these items into the hamper. After removing, inspect for stains or soil, shake, then hang to be worn again. Not only does this cut down on the amount of laundry, it extends the life of the garment.

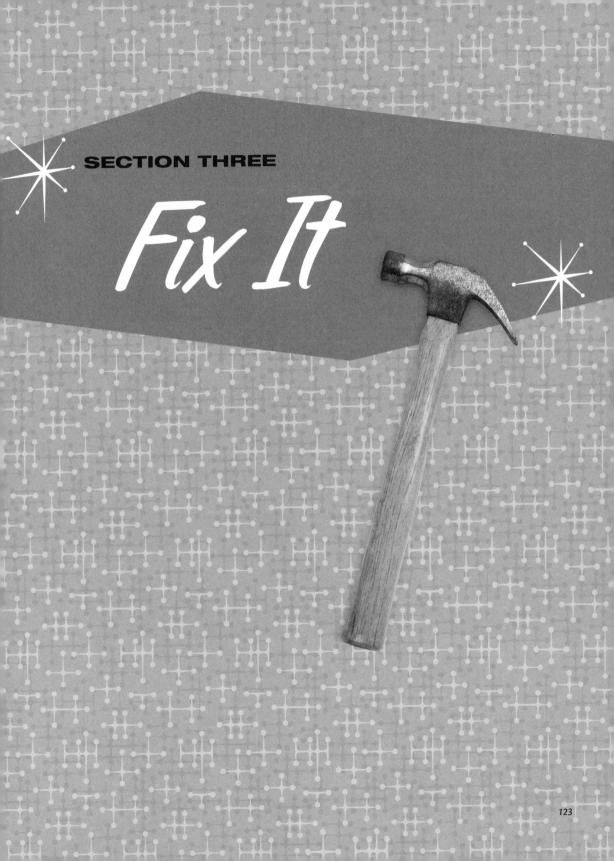

SECTION THREE

Fix It

TWELVE

The Bare Minimum Handyman Guide

You may think *handyman* or *handywoman* is the last word that describes you, and that's fine. But there is a baseline for self-sufficiency, meaning that whether you live in a house or an apartment, there are a few tools and concepts you must be familiar with, even before unpacking. These are the nonnegotiable skills even children should be taught and given a chance to practice, in case of emergency. So this chapter applies to you, even if you plan to never lift a hammer or a screwdriver in your lifetime.

Maintenance Isn't Optional

Would further neglect cause further damage or potential injury? Frayed cords, leaky pipes, holes in the roof, and trip hazards must be addressed immediately, even with an ugly temporary solution if necessary.

Electrical Hazards

Neglecting a potential electrical hazard is comparable to dropping a lit match on the carpet and hoping it doesn't catch. Periodically inspect cords for fraying, especially near the plug, where improper use can cause

Basic Tools to Have On Hand

To minimize property damage and ensure safety, every household should have a basic toolkit, even if the mailbox doesn't read Mr. or Ms. Handyman. Remember, not all of these items need to be stored together—it's not necessary to keep the plunger and drain snake with your screwdriver.

- hammer
- screwdriver with interchangeable tips
- assorted fasteners (these are sold in inexpensive kits, with lots of brad nails, small hooks, nails, screws, for many minor repairs and improvements)
- adjustable wrenches, a.k.a., a crescent wrench
- slip-joint pliers, often referred to as channel locks
- needle-nose pliers
- noncontact voltage detector (available in the electrical aisle of most hardware stores)
- duct tape
- level
- gloves
- drain plunger
- toilet plunger
- drain snake
- tarp

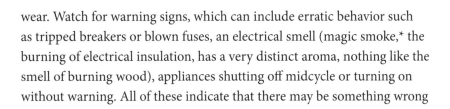

wear. Watch for warning signs, which can include erratic behavior such as tripped breakers or blown fuses, an electrical smell (magic smoke,* the burning of electrical insulation, has a very distinct aroma, nothing like the smell of burning wood), appliances shutting off midcycle or turning on without warning. All of these indicate that there may be something wrong

---

* No, not the magic smoke from your college days.

with the wiring. If you encounter any of these problems, shut off power to the appliance and inspect the cord. If the appliance appears beyond repair, cut the cord and dispose of the appliance properly. Removing the cord prevents a potentially dangerous appliance from being scavenged for reuse.

Water

When plumbing issues arise, the most important thing to do is to stop the water from coming into the house or, in the case of a sewage back up, remove the water as expeditiously as possible. Whether a home is a rental or not, it is imperative to know how to turn off the water. In an apartment complex, the water main is usually for the entire building, but typically there is a valve under each sink, near the water heater, and behind each toilet. While damage to an apartment may be more of the landlord's concern, consider that the cleanup may cause a significant inconvenience for you and it would be best to minimize the damage, if at all possible. In most modern detached homes, the water main is usually located at the meter, which can be in the yard, near the street, or at the point where the water line enters the home, often in a basement.

After the water is no longer coming in, it's important to remove the water as expeditiously as possible because drywall and wood can quickly become waterlogged mold farms. In extreme situations, it is best to call in a professional for water and sewage removal. They have high power vacuums that will out-suck all but Tim "The Toolman" Taylor's shop vac. For small-scale overflows, a wet-dry shop vac should do the job.

After you have removed the water, run fans or a dehumidifier until the room's humidity has returned to normal. Normal humidity levels vary based on climate, but optimal is around 50 percent.

Learn how to plunge a toilet (chapter 14). It's always embarrassing if a toilet becomes plugged and you were the last to use it, especially if you are a guest in someone's home when it happens. It's significantly less awkward to ask for a plunger than to have a homeowner deal with your mess.

Confession

Once, in my apartment days, I awoke to the sound of my roommate pounding on her bedroom door, from the inside. The doorknob had jammed and she was locked in her room. As we didn't have so much as a screwdriver, I had to face the maintenance man and beg him to let my friend out. He laughed at us the entire time. Entire countries lost for the sake of nail; my pride for the sake of a screwdriver.

The Elements

It's pretty easy to let household maintenance slide, but an ounce of prevention will stop emergencies from cropping up. Clean your gutters each spring and each fall. Replace missing downspout diverters to keep rain from causing damp and moldy basements or crawlspaces.

Check your foundation regularly. Gaps in the foundation or around entryways are open invitations to drafts and pests that can range from bugs to snakes to rodents, depending on the size of the gaps. Repair these as they are discovered to keep heating bills low and pesky squatters out.*

If your region has termites, and many do, the bond and annual inspection are not an option. Sure, the money may be difficult to pull together, but it could save tens of thousands of dollars long term.

In colder climates, shovel and salt snowy walkways and stairs to prevent slips and falls. Better an hour of shoveling than weeks of physical therapy. Choose a wide snow shovel and use it to push the snow into piles at the edges of your walkways. Don't dig in the snow like it's dirt. After the path is clear, sprinkle it generously with salt to prevent ice from forming. Clear paths as soon as possible because half-melted snow is heavier, and if it refreezes, a layer of ice will form above and below the snow, making it much more hazardous and nearly impossible to move.

---

* If "pesky squatters" also includes your brother-in-law, more dramatic measures are called for.

Fixing a Finish

Dear Home-Ec 101,

My daughter spilled fingernail polish remover on her dresser. What can I do to repair it?

Signed,

Acetone ACK!

There are a few options to make the best of the situation. First, we have the disguise-it–and-pretend-it-didn't-happen approach. With this method, you clean up any remaining acetone and find a knickknack or doily to place over the damaged area. This is hands down my favorite approach for damage-prone furniture, such as pieces that live in a child's room. Then again, how many ten-year-olds like doilies? It only works so well.

A more costly approach is to call the manufacturer and ask if they offer repair services. Even if they don't, they may be able to provide the color of the stain and the type of the finish, which will aid in repairing the piece yourself.

Time, sunlight, and humidity all take a toll on furniture and gradually change the coloration, so making a perfect match on an old dresser is unlikely, but the repair can be disguised. If the damaged area is small, consider a specialized pen that stains dents and dings to hide the bare wood. Look for these in the paint and stain section of hardware and big-box stores. For larger areas, sand and use a matching stain, followed by the appropriate finish to match the rest of the piece. Follow the manufacturer's stain and finish recommendations for the best results.

Last is the shabby-chic solution: Strip the dresser, repaint it, and embrace the imperfection.

Set the Bar Lower

If you are just starting out in your first apartment or home, or if your home is full of young children (or soon will be), save money and stress by buying used furniture. When that first water ring, nick, or errant crayon marking appears (it will happen), you'll be less likely to freak out and it will just add to the character of the piece. Estate and moving sales are great places to look. If yard sales aren't an option, check the scratch-and-dent section of the furniture store (it's often hidden in the back corner). Ensure the flaw doesn't destroy the warranty, unless of course the savings outweigh the benefit.

The same scratch-and-dent principle holds true for appliances: A dented washer cleans just as well as a pristine appliance. Another option is to consider factory refurbished models. These are appliances that have been returned for some reason, not necessarily due to defect. Each appliance is fixed and inspected before being sold at a significant reduction in price, occasionally with a warranty.

Showcase homes are a sham. Sure, they are gorgeous, but like a glossy magazine, it's not the reality of everyday life. Once a home is lived in, the scuffs, dings, and dirt move in, too. Wipe away the smudges, repair large holes as they occur, but realize that repainting shouldn't be a seasonal undertaking. It is the occupant who is most aware of imperfections. Repair items as needed, but life is too short to be a slave to possessions. Accept some of the wear as physical evidence of the memories made in a home.

Basic Safety and Property Care

First, locate and test each and every smoke and/or carbon monoxide detector. In newer construction, fire codes mandate that a smoke detector be installed and functional at minimum on each level of a home, in bedrooms, and in the garage. Replace all the batteries as soon as you move in. You don't know how old the current batteries are. Then test your batteries twice a year. Many people do this on the first and last days of daylight saving time because it's easy to remember.

Locate the fire extinguisher and ensure it is in working order. By law, the instructions for use must be printed on or attached to the device. Fire extinguishers have an expiration date. When the expiration date has passed, it is time to replace the apparatus. If you have never operated one, use the old one to practice, outside.

Remember to always treat kitchen fires as though they are grease fires, unless the source is obvious. Never use water on a grease or electrical fire—in both cases water exacerbates the situation. A manageable fire can be spread if splashed. In the case of an electrical fire, immediately shut off the power by flipping the main breaker. If a fire extinguisher is not available in the case of a grease fire, cover the flames with a lid if the fire is in a pan or smother the fire with salt or baking soda if it is on the counter or stove. Do not attempt this with flour, which is highly flammable.

Never use water on a grease or electrical fire.

Natural Gas

If your home uses natural gas for heating or operating appliances, you must be able to turn off the gas in case of a leak or a natural disaster such as an earthquake. Renters should have the landlord demonstrate the valve's operation. When a natural gas leak is suspected, shut off the main valve, and exit the premises, then call in a professional.

Circuit Breakers and Fuse Boxes

Locate the circuit breaker or fuse box and become familiar with its layout and operation. Make sure it is properly labeled—each breaker or fuse should name which room it controls. You know you've tripped a breaker or blown a fuse if the power goes out in one area of the house but not the others. You've probably overloaded a power outlet by plugging too many devices into it at once. Unplug some devices, then go to the breaker box. The tripped breaker will be halfway between the off and on positions. Switch it back to the on position to restore power. Use fewer devices at the same time (or in the same room) to avoid tripping the breaker again. If the breaker box is located in a garage or basement, make sure that the surrounding area is not used for storage. The box must be accessible at all times. No excuses.

On a less serious note, all automatic garage door openers have a safety release. Sorry if it bursts any bubbles, but a convenient power outage is no excuse for calling off of work. Simply pull the release to disengage the chain. Then lift the door, like Grandma had to. It's not as fun as a day off, but it's better than being thought an ignoramus.

Leaks and Broken Windows

Even the most fumbling person has the ability to at least reduce future damage when a minor household crisis occurs. With broken windows or damaged roofing, keeping the elements out is the top priority. This is where your tarp and a few nails will come in handy.

Windows and doors that don't secure properly are a flashing *open* sign for petty thieves. Homes that advertise their lack of security are considered low-hanging fruit. Also, ensure your home has adequate outdoor lighting and replace light bulbs as soon as they burn out. Energy-efficient bulbs that have longer life spans will keep changes to a minimum. Consider installing motion-detecting lights. Trim hedges that may obscure windows and entry-ways, as these provide cover for a would-be intruder.

THIRTEEN

When Good Appliances Go Bad: Avoid Minor Meltdowns

Unexpected appliance failure is one of life's more irksome experiences. If you had seen it coming, you could have done something to limit the impact, such as preventative maintenance, a dedicated replacement fund, or applied duct tape. Fortunately, as humans we have been blessed with the ability to use tools,* not the least of which resides comfortably between one's ears, provided that it has been loaded with a little basic knowledge.

Listing specific guidelines for troubleshooting every home appliance (and make and model) would make this chapter thicker than the average politician. Instead, this chapter covers basic troubleshooting, which will solve simple problems, point you in the general direction for further research, or allow you to accurately describe the situation to a professional repair person. Most appliances have the make—or brand—visible on the outside of the unit. The model number may be more difficult to find. It could be on the inside of a door or on the back of the appliance. Using the make and model, it is possible to find almost any manual online for free, or for a small fee, if it is a vintage version.

* Hurray for opposable digits!

Average Life Spans for Major Appliances

Appliance	Life Span (in years)*
Air Conditioner (Central)	15
Heater, Forced Air, Electric	15–35
Heater, Forced Air, Gas/Oil	15–35
Heater, Baseboard	15–25
Water Heater, Gas	12
Water Heater, Electric	13
Dishwasher	10
Electric Range	17
Gas Range	19
Garbage Disposal	10
Refrigerator	5–25
Washer, Top Load	13
Washer, Front Load	11
Dryer	14

* These are estimates. The life span will vary based on model, care and maintenance, and usage.

Before You Begin

- If the device is electrical, unplug it or turn off the breaker.
- If the device is gas-powered, turn off the gas.
- If the device is nuclear, put down this book—there is a United Nations Inspector at your door.

If a home has appliances that run on natural gas, familiarize yourself with lighting the pilot light for each appliance. A service call just to find out that the pilot is out is a double blow: first to one's pride and second to the wallet.

Heating and Cooling Systems

Heating and cooling systems are high-dollar investments that require routine maintenance to run efficiently and to live out their expected life span. A professional should be consulted for most repairs and for regular inspections as required by the warranty or service agreement. Still, there are a few routine chores that anyone can do. Regularly check and replace the air filter for central air, heat pumps, and forced air heaters; a clogged filter stresses the compressor, which can dramatically increase the utility bill.

Recirculated water heating systems have a water pump that requires greasing annually. While these heating systems are low maintenance, air can build up in the pipes. Each radiator has a valve that can be opened to release the trapped air. If this isn't done from time

Never block the intake of a forced-air furnace or air-conditioning unit. This will create a strain on the system, reducing its life span.

to time, the amount of hot water warming the room will slowly diminish, reducing the efficiency of the system.

Hot Water Heaters

Whether gas, electric, or tankless, all water heaters must be flushed from time to time. All water has mineral content or sediment that flows into the home. With the hot water heater being the point of entry for a large portion of the water, the sediment buildup can be significant.

Flush standard tank heaters annually. Grab a garden hose and a bucket. Turn off the power to the hot water heater. If the unit is a gas appliance, turn the heat all the way down to conserve energy during the process. Near the bottom of the tank is a panel. Open the panel and attach the garden hose to the spigot. Run the hose to an area where the water can safely drain. Please be aware that the water will be hot unless the unit has been off for some time. Open the valve and allow the water to drain for five minutes. After the time has elapsed, catch the draining water in a bucket and examine for sediment. If there is grit or sand, allow the water to flush for an additional five minutes. Repeat until the water is clear, then turn off the valve, remove the garden hose, and restore power to the appliance.

Tankless water heaters must also be flushed annually, but you will want to hire a professional to do it unless you had service valves installed with your unit. If so, consult the owner's manual for instructions on how to flush the system. If the unit isn't flushed, scaling from dissolved minerals may build up on the coils that heat the water, reducing the unit's efficiency.

Refrigerators
Refrigerators are notorious for causing unnecessary service calls. When a refrigerator isn't efficiently keeping food cool, the impact on the utility bill is noticeable.

If your refrigerator doesn't seem to be doing its job, try these solutions before you call a professional:

- Is the door closed all the way? Sounds silly, right? Sometimes the crisper or meat drawer isn't quite closed and this prevents the main door from closing tightly and maintaining a good seal.
- Check the settings. Sometimes house elves turn the dials all the way down, just for giggles, I guess.
- Check the gasket, or rubber seal around the door. If the gasket has pulled away from the door, it may only need to be pushed back into place. If it shows signs of damage, take the make and model number to a nearby appliance repair store and get a replacement.
- Check the coils. If the coils are coated in a thick layer of dust, the refrigerator won't run efficiently. Give them a good vacuuming as described in chapter 4.

If a refrigerator is not cooling efficiently and none of the problems listed above are present, it may be an issue with the thermostat or the appliance may be low on refrigerant. These problems are for experienced DIYers or a professional.

Garbage Disposals

Despite the insistence of urban legends, there are no sharp knives lurking in the bowels of the disposal. The unit actually has dull blades that grind, rather than slice, the food into bits small enough to be flushed down the drain. From time to time a small piece of bone, plastic, or a fork becomes jammed under the blade, preventing movement. If this happens, immediately turn off the power. Allowing the motor to strain will damage the appliance and significantly reduce its life span.

Once the power has been switched off, preferably at the breaker, it is safe to address the source of the problem. On occasion, broken glass finds its way into a disposal or a bone is splintered by the appliance, and it is for these reasons, and not for the actual blades, that gloves are suggested. Use rubber gloves to protect your hand and reach into the unit to clear out any loose debris or random utensil from the disposal. If the blades do not turn freely once the loose debris has been cleared, look at the very bottom of the appliance, under the sink. Most models have a small nut that can be turned with an allen wrench. Wiggle this nut until the offending debris is released.

After the blades have been freed, it may be necessary to press a reset button, which will be located somewhere on the underside of the unit. Restore power to the machine and test it with the water running.

Garbage disposals are notorious for developing a funky odor, but usually it's a pretty simple fix. When the disposal runs, it frequently splashes pulverized food debris onto the walls of the drain pipe. If this food isn't flushed away with plenty of water during the operation of the machine, it will begin to smell. After operating the disposal, plug the drain and fill the sink with a few quarts of hot, soapy water. Pull the plug on the drain and run the disposal to flush all the food particles down the drain.

If a smell has developed, further measures may be necessary. Toss the peel from half a lemon or orange into the sink, add a handful of salt, and turn the unit on while running the hot water. After these items have worked their way into the drain, turn off the disposal, fill the sink with hot, soapy water, and run the disposal while draining.

Dishwasher*

Despite the shiny exterior and fancy buttons, the dishwasher is a very simple machine comprised of a water pump, heating element, control panel, and solenoids.

The dishwasher is leaking. Inspect the rubber gasket, the squishy rubber part around the door that ensures it seals tightly. If the gasket has rotted, become loose, or has chunks bitten out by a certain two-year-old, replace the gasket. Visit your nearest appliance parts store with the make and model of your appliance. They will happily help you find the correct part.

Solenoids aren't scary, they are simply magnetic plungers that open and shut valves.

Most built-in dishwashers are screwed into the cabinetry with only a few screws. Remove these to move the unit and check the water lines to and from the appliance. If the lines are cracked or coming loose, tighten or replace them as needed.

If neither the gasket nor the water lines are the problem, the tub itself may be cracked. This is not an easily replaced part, so don't be surprised if you need a new unit.

The dishwasher fills but does not drain. Built-in dishwashers typically connect to and drain into the garbage disposal or the kitchen sink's drain line. If the kitchen sink is clogged, the dishwasher will not drain. Clear the

* Handy Midwestern translation: dishwoarscher

kitchen drain and inspect the drain line that runs from the dishwasher to the sink. Additionally, check and clean the debris screen of the dishwasher itself.

The dishwasher runs but does not fill. Look inside the bottom of the washtub for a light plastic piece resembling a plastic cup. This is the float. It may be stuck in the up position, telling the machine it is full. Remove the petrified french fry or other debris and the float should move freely, allowing the unit to fill. Running a dishwasher without water will overheat the motor, possibly causing permanent damage.

If hard water is a problem in your area, adding citric acid to the wash cycle can dramatically improve the cleaning power of your dishwasher.

The dishwasher sounds like it is chewing on broken glass. Check for any silverware flying around in the machine. If everything is securely in place and the washer arms are not banging into anything, one of the bearings in the motor may be damaged and the unit will soon fail. Start saving.

The dishwasher is no longer cleaning dishes well. Examine the spray arm. If the holes are clogged with mineral deposits, soak the arm in diluted vinegar and use a pipe cleaner or safety pin to clean out any gunk.

Clothes Dryer

Dryers are very simple appliances. Think of them as heaters that happen to tumble your clothing. If the appliance runs but doesn't dry the clothes well, check the lint filter and the vent. If the damp air can't easily exit the machine, clothes may not dry well, and a clogged vent is a fire hazard.

If the dryer gets hot, but the drum won't turn, it is likely a broken belt or pulley. The machine will have to be opened, which usually is only a matter of removing a few screws. If a belt or pulley is the cause, it will need to be replaced. Search online for the manual of the dryer and contact an appliance store to obtain the correct parts. The manual should have a clear explanation for replacement.

If the drum turns but the dryer does not heat, the heating element or the thermostat is probably the culprit. Replace the parts as necessary.

Clothes Washer

Don't be afraid to disassemble your washer before calling in a repair person. Depending on the model, it may be the only way to access certain hoses. Consult the owner's manual for your particular model; some washers may open from the top, others from the side, and a few only from the back. Use a putty knife wrapped in electrical tape to prevent scratching the finish, and do not use force.

Washer won't drain. Check the drain hose. It may be full of lint, debris, or a small item such as a baby's sock. All washers have an in-line filter.

Water is leaking from the washer. Check the hose connections, both from the wall and to the appliance. Also, check the drain hose. If the washer is a front loader, check the gasket that seals the door; if there are cracks, or pieces missing, it may need to be replaced. Look for areas of corrosion around the outside of the tub.

Burning or electrical odor. Unplug the washer and try to isolate the source. It could be the control panel or

If fabric softener or dryer sheets are used in the home, occasionally wash the dryer's lint trap with soap and water. Use a nailbrush to clean the screen well. A film of softener can develop over time, reducing airflow and efficiency.

motor; in either case, you'll probably need to replace the part. Don't plug in the machine until it has been repaired.

Vacuum Cleaners

Show of hands: When is the last time you took a good look at your vacuum's beater bar or brush? Thought so. This *should* be done after every vacuuming. Every so often, grab a utility knife and screw driver, unplug the vacuum, and flip it over so the beater bar is visible. Depending on the model of the vacuum, it may be necessary to remove the cover to improve access to the bar. Use the utility knife to cut away all of the hair, fur, and string that has wrapped itself around the agitator. When the bristles are clogged, they cannot separate the carpet fibers, which impedes the vacuum's ability to suck. If anyone in the household has long hair, this chore should be done frequently to prevent damage to the belt.

Some vacuum models need to have the belt replaced seasonally. As the belt becomes worn, it stretches and begins to slip, turning the agitator less efficiently. Usually the belt is very simple to replace, requiring only a screwdriver or two. New belts can often be found in box stores, but if the belt is for an uncommon model, it may be necessary to order it online or to visit a vacuum supply store. Buy several belts, in case one breaks just when the in-laws have called to say they are on their way.

Vacuums can lose suction for several reasons. On bagged models, the most common reason is a full bag. A bag should be replaced when it is 80 percent full because as the debris collects, the power of the vacuum reduces until the act of running the vacuum becomes merely an exercise in noise creation.

Operator Error

Vacuuming can be a great life metaphor. Everyone has faced the stubborn scrap of paper dilemma: You pass the vacuum head over it again and again, but somehow it eludes the suction. Deep down you know it would be simpler to bend over and pick up the paper, but still you try again. Sometimes people go one step further: They pick up the scrap, give it a good look, and put it back just to give the vacuum one last chance. Perhaps it is the tool operating the vacuum that should be checked.

Know the Model Number

When purchasing a new belt, bring the old belt and the model number of the vacuum to prevent a second trip to the store.

With bagless models, a dirty filter may be the culprit. If the filter is a paper cartridge, it can be replaced for a nominal price. Spongelike filters be can rinsed under running water and allowed to dry thoroughly before replacing.

Sometimes a small item, like a kid's toy, can become lodged in one of the hoses. If the hose is straight, a broom handle can usually push the clog through. If the hose bends, bend the tip of a wire coat hanger back on itself to form a small hook. Feed the hanger through the bend in the hose and push it all the way through. Don't pull the hanger back or it may snag and rip the hose.

Remember, with all appliances, a little maintenance can go a long way to extending the life span.

FOURTEEN

Plumbing: Someone Jiggle the Handle Already

It doesn't take a mustache or sexy green or red coveralls to wield a pipe wrench,* but sturdy gloves and old clothes do come in handy, as does a compromised sense of smell and an eight-bit soundtrack. In this chapter, you'll learn the basics of removing clogs and fixing minor toilet issues.

Toilets

Toilets are usually basic fixtures. They utilize gravity to move waste into the sewage system, and despite popular sentiment, they do not lead to the ocean. Water flows into the tank through an inlet valve to fill the reservoir (usually there is a knob behind the toilet that can be turned off to keep water from flowing into the reservoir). A float on the inside of the tank turns the water off when it reaches the proper level, and an overflow drain keeps water from pouring out of the tank if the float malfunctions. On the outside of the tank is a handle used to move a trip lever inside the tank. The trip lever pulls a chain that is attached to a flap. When the flap is raised, water pours into the toilet bowl, which will fill until there is a large enough volume of

* I'm looking at you, Mario and Luigi.

Plumbing Equipment

Here are the basic tools you need on hand for minor plumbing issues.

Sink plunger: Is shaped like a ball cut in half. The flat bottom forms a seal in sinks and tubs.

Toilet plunger: Shaped like a bell with a narrow cup at the bottom. The cup fits into the hole at the base of the bowl, making a more effective seal.

Plumber's snake: A flexible metal auger, usually made of coiled wire, designed to remove clogs. Unlike a plunger or compressed air, the snake comes in direct contact with a clog.

Pipe wrench: Bigger and sturdier than a standard wrench, a pipe wrench has adjustable jaws and a long handle to give more torque (power) in use.

Bucket: You really don't want to catch what comes out of drain pipes in a bowl. Really.

water to move waste past the trap and into the sewage line. This usually runs smoothly, unless a clog blocks the flow. If a toilet is overflowing due to a clog in the pipe, turn off the water at the inlet valve under the tank. If there is no inlet valve, take the lid off the tank and lift the float up to stop the flow of water. Then grab a toilet plunger and attack the clog.

A toilet plunger is designed to increase pressure enough to pull a small clog apart or push it past the bend in the pipe to the wider line. To operate a plunger, place the smaller cup into the drain of the toilet and try to form a seal with the lip of the plunger. With moderate force, press down on the plunger (don't go crazy or you'll slosh the water). The additional pressure is often all that is needed to force the obstruction along. However, it may take several tries, and a good seal is important. A little Barry White playing in the background may help set the mood.

Force the Flush

If there is no running water, a toilet can usually be flushed with a bucket of water poured into the bowl. Be aware that some municipalities have power-assisted sewage systems that may not function in an extended blackout.

Low Flow Woe

In 1994, the maximum gallons per flush was reduced from 3.5 to 1.6 gallons, and while the new toilets saved water, they made a lot of owners unhappy. If you are the proud owner of a toilet made in the mid- to late-nineties, expect to reach for the plunger on occasion. It took a few years to get the design down to an art. Sediment can collect in the traps of these low-flow toilets, making flushing even more difficult, but a good plunge can push things along their way.

On the other hand, if the toilet in your home is from a previous era, it's possible to reduce the gallons per flush by placing a plastic bottle full of water in the tank. Just make sure that the bottle does not interfere with the float and won't block the flap's operation. This simple act can create a significant positive impact on a home's yearly water bill.

Clogs

The best way to deal with serious clogs is to prevent them in the first place. Never flush anything other than waste and toilet paper. Keep a trash can in the restroom for all other waste products. Contrary to popular belief, facial tissue, feminine products, cigarette butts, prophylactics, and expired medications are not harmless to flush.

Toilet paper is designed to fall apart in water, but too much can create a clog—usually a plunger is enough to move things along. More serious clogs, often caused by feminine products or other items that are not sewage-friendly may require a plumbing snake to break them up. It's nasty, but so is the bill from a plumber. Feed the end of the snake into the drain until you meet resistance, then turn the crank and push on the snake in the direction of the clog. The turning allows the wire to twist around the bends in the pipe or to work at the clog itself. Remember, a clog may be past the first bend in the pipe. If the water level doesn't sink, continue feeding wire into the drain until the next area of resistance is met. If a plumbing snake isn't available, a wire coat hanger can be used, but it takes a little finesse. Unbend the hanger until the whole thing is straight except for a small hook on the end. Gently feed the hanger down the drain and twist it as you feed it into the line. A hanger doesn't bend and twist as easily as a plumbing snake. Expect some difficulty maneuvering it around the trap.

Leaky Seals

Bleach is murder on plastic. Remember that the next time a drop-in toilet cleaning tablet looks tempting. Many drop-in toilet cleaners rely on chlorine bleach to kill germs, but the internal workings of toilets rely on rubber and plastic. Over time, exposure to bleach causes the flap to become brittle, which allows water to seep past the seal. The good news is the plumbing aisle of every hardware store has replacement toilet innards, cheap.

To check for a leaky seal, remove the tank lid and add a few drops of food coloring to the water. Replace the lid and check the bowl after a few hours. (Make sure no one has used or flushed the toilet in the meantime). If there is any colored water in the bowl, the flap should be replaced.

Water Seals

Modern building codes require plumbing fixtures to have a trap (which is simply a special bend) in the pipe to keep a water seal between the fixture (for example, a toilet or sink) and the sewage line. The water seal is simply the water that is trapped in the bend between the sewer line and the fixture. Sewage gas is serious business. Methane and other harmful gases could enter a home if it weren't for the water seal. If a bathroom is unused most of the time, occasionally run water into the drain to prevent the seal from evaporating.

The Howling Toilet Mystery

Dear Home-Ec 101,

I awoke the other night as I heard the most awful noise coming from my bathroom. It was coming from the toilet. My husband swears I'm nuts, but the toilet was howling. What would cause this?

Signed,

Toilet Terror

You aren't crazy and I remember this happening once when I was a kid. Inside the tank is a part referred to as a ballcock,* that's the whole float, arm, and valve setup. The howling is caused by the vibration of water trying to seep into the toilet. Replacing the float and flapper setup in your toilet will exorcise the demon from your bathroom.**

* Nah, way too easy.

** But may not restore your appetite for split pea soup.

The Case of the Constantly Running Toilet

The chain that attaches the flush handle to the flap can sag or break, which will prevent the flap from making a good seal. A twist tie or paper clip can work as a temporary fix if the chain should break entirely. Sometimes the chain is too short, which will keep the flap from sitting securely over the drain; a flap that doesn't seal can leak, and a slow trickle over time can significantly impact your water bill. If the chain is fine, check the flap for corrosion or grime. Either one can prevent a good seal. In these cases, cleaning or replacing the flap should solve the problem.

Sometimes the float can become stuck, which will prevent the float from shutting off the inlet valve. If the float looks like a plastic or metal balloon, make sure the arm or rod it is connected to is straight. In this position, the float should sit lightly on top of the water. If it doesn't, the float could have a leak, and in that case you need to replace it. If the float looks more like a cup attached to a rod, try manipulating the float to see if it is stuck in position. The solution may be as simple as removing a piece of grit.

If This Toilet's Rocking, There's a Problem

Underneath the commode, or base of the toilet, is a large wax ring that acts as both a seal around the sewage pipe and as a cushion. Imagine 180 pounds of person coming in for a landing several times a day—a wax pillow would be nice. Over time, the wax seal breaks down, or worse, leaks. Replacing the seal isn't a difficult job, but the toilet itself is quite heavy. Keep this in mind before choosing to fly solo. Sometimes it's not the seal, but the bolts that attach the toilet to the floor. Always check these before assuming the wax seal is bad. While down there checking the bolts, examine the integrity of the floor. If there is water damage, you'll have to remove the toilet and repair the flooring before further damage occurs.

Turn the water off at the inlet valve, flush the toilet, and hold the handle down until all of the water has drained into the bowl. Plunge any remaining water down the drain. Inside the tank are two bolts that secure it to the base. First disconnect the water, then unscrew the tank and set it aside. The base of the toilet is bolted to the floor. Look for two cap-covered bolts (usually on either side of the base) and remove the nuts before attempting to lift the base. Remove the base and set it aside. You will see the wax seal around

Tree Roots in the Pipes

Sometimes tree roots find their way into sewage pipes. Once there, they grow like crazy, blocking the pipe and causing sewage to back up into a home. This is a project for seasoned DIYers or professionals.

Install an In-Line Shutoff Valve

In some areas, new tract or spec homes are being built without in-line shutoff valves. These can be installed at low cost and eliminate the need to shut off the water main for minor repairs.

the sewage pipe. A new seal can be purchased quite inexpensively, and this is not a place to skimp. (After all, it's not exactly the most pleasant way to spend an afternoon.) Follow the directions on the box, return the base to its former position, and tighten the bolts. Before reattaching the tank, it may be a good idea to pour water down the commode to see if the new seal is watertight before going any further. If no water seeps out, replace the tank, tighten the bolts, then reattach the waterline before opening the valve to refill the tank. If one of the bolts under the tank leaks after tightening, try adding a new gasket (which looks like a small plastic washer) under it.

Unclogging Sinks, Tubs, and Showers

Slow drains are often the result of hair and the buildup of other funk reducing the width of the pipe. Chemical drain cleaners are readily available and can break down organic clogs without damaging the pipe. The problem with these chemicals is they are dangerous and cause chemical burns, and if splashed into eyes they can cause blindness. If children are present in a home, consider other options.

Caustic describes chemicals with a high pH like bleach.

Kitchen Sinks

Two rules to remember: Never pour grease down a drain, and flush the drain occasionally with very hot (near boiling) water. Sinks can also be plunged, like a toilet. If the kitchen has a double sink (meaning there are two drains), the second drain must be blocked tightly during plunging or the plunger will be ineffective. Make sure the plug is held in place while plunging or it may fly out of the drain with some force. When plunging a double sink with a disposal, only plunge the side without the disposal. For an extra good seal, a layer of petroleum jelly can be applied to the lip of the plunger. Be sure to run lots of water to flush any debris away.

Bathroom Sinks

Hair-wrapped stoppers are a primary cause of slow-draining bathroom sinks. The stoppers grab hair and other goo before it can be washed away. Under the sink, where the pipe exits the bowl, is a nut on the back side of the drain pipe. This attaches the control arm to the stopper. Place a bucket under the work area and wear gloves. Loosen and remove the nut to slide the control arm away from the pipe. Once the control arm is clear, the stopper should pull right out and drag all of its nasty yuck with it. Be forewarned, this bacterial playground is going to smell. Discard the mess and rinse off the stopper—in another sink. It'd be wise to clean the goo out of the pipe as well. A bottlebrush comes in handy for this task, but an old toothbrush works, too; the bucket should catch any spillage. Finally, reassemble everything and be sure to tighten the nut around the control arm to prevent leaks.

Common Causes of Clogs

There are some usual suspects when it comes to clogged drains. In the kitchen, grease and food particles top the list. Never put pasta, flour, or starchy vegetables down the drain. These swell in water and can create quite the mess.

Hair, body oil, soap scum, and toothpaste are frequent offenders in bathrooms. Flush your drains from time to time with very hot water to help rinse away buildup.

Retrieving Items Dropped Down the Drain

While not every sink has a stopper, in modern buildings sinks have a P- or J-style trap whose primary role is to create a water seal to keep sewage gas out (see the sidebar on page 145). The sink traps have a handy secondary function—they can catch small solid objects dropped down the drain, such as rings and jewelry. To access the trap, grab a bucket and a pipe wrench. Loosen the nut at the joint by turning it counter-clockwise. Do this at each end of the J-shaped section. Make sure the bucket is beneath the trap and carefully pull the section away from the other pipe. Allow the water to spill into the bucket before inspecting the pipe for the missing or offending object. Unless the water was running at full force, solid objects will settle in the trap, along with sand and other sediment.

Be careful not to use too much force when working with PVC pipe; it can crack.

Bathtubs and Showers

To clear hair clogs from a bathtub, use a screwdriver to remove the plate covering the overflow drain. The overflow drain will usually be in the wall of the tub below the faucet and over the drain. If someone leaves the tub running, the overflow prevents water from running over the top of the tub. Use a rag to tightly block the opening of the overflow drain to maintain the pressure. Skipping this step renders plunging ineffective. Once the overflow drain is completely plugged, use a sink plunger to move the clog along. Hair clogs can be very stubborn, and may require a plumber's snake to fix. Remove the rag from the overflow drain and feed the snake through the overflow pipe. It will join the tub's drain. Gently feed the snake until the obstruction is met and the clog breaks up. Then flush the pipe with lots of very hot water, which will help rinse away body oil and soap scum. Yum.

Clearing a shower clog is the same as unclogging a tub, except the drain cover needs to be removed and there is no overflow to worry about. Often hair clogs in a shower drain settle quite far down the line. Use patience when snaking the pipe. You may need to work past a bend.

Sewage Backups

Once in a while a clog occurs between a home and the main sewage line. The first clue is often sewage backing up into the lowest drains in the house—typically a first-floor or basement shower or toilet. Immediately turn off all water. Make sure the washer and dishwasher are turned off. Anything that drains into the sewage line will only exacerbate the problem. These clogs are often caused by tree roots. In subdivisions, if the clog happens after one home's sewage line joins with its neighbors, it is a municipal sewage problem. Ask your neighbors to shut off their water as well and call the water/sewer company. If the clog is in the pipe leading from the municipal line to the house, the home owner is responsible for the repair and it's time to call in a professional.

FIFTEEN

Throw Rugs and Posters Only Go So Far: Fixing Floors and Walls

Dents and dings happen, and once you're out of college, careful poster arrangement won't cut it; actual repair is a must. The vast majority of interior walls are Sheetrock or drywall,* which is plaster or gypsum sandwiched between paper. The boards are screwed to the frame of the house and the joints are hidden with drywall compound. With the exception of water damage, most drywall repair is quite simple and inexpensive. Most drywall damage falls into one of the following categories.

Small Holes

Tools you'll need: Utility knife, putty knife, drywall compound, fine-grain sandpaper.

Use the utility knife to cut away any jagged edges and to shape the hole so the edges are sloped. This technique increases the surface area on which the drywall compound can adhere. Apply the compound in layers, no more than $\frac{1}{8}$-inch (3mm) thick, allowing it to dry fully between applications. Use the putty knife both to apply the compound and to scrape away

---

* If your walls are paneling, it's time to move out of the basement and get your own place. "Bye Mom!"

excess. It's best to apply the compound until it is slightly higher than the surrounding wall. The excess should be sanded away and the patch painted to match.

Nail Pops

Tools you'll need: Drywall screws, drywall compound, putty knife, drill or screwdriver, fine-grain sandpaper.

To prevent nail pops from reoccurring, the Sheetrock must be secured. Add a new drywall screw to the stud 2 to 3 inches (5cm to 8cm) above and below the one that has worked itself loose. Remove the popped screw or use another nail and hammer to tap it $1/16$-inch (1mm) below the surface of the wall (this is called countersinking). Don't hammer directly on Sheetrock; the force will dent the surrounding drywall and you'll run the risk of creating cracks. Fill the depression with drywall compound, following the same directions used to repair small holes.

Large Holes

Tools you'll need: Keyhole saw, thin wood strips, mesh tape, drywall patch, drywall screws, drywall compound, putty knife, fine-grain sandpaper.

Holes up to 3-inches (8cm) in diameter can be repaired with a mesh repair kit, but larger holes require more effort. For large holes, use a template to trace a square around the damaged area, then use a keyhole saw to cut away the damaged drywall. Before cutting, ensure no plumbing or wiring is located behind the damaged area.

Flat Finish Paint

When choosing paint for walls with significant repair work, flat finishes do a much better job hiding imperfections, but not all flat paint is washable, and this finish will need to be dusted frequently and re-painted more often to avoid a grimy look.

Because it's rare to get a peek behind the walls, it's a good idea to look for pest damage or lost cultural treasures* while the hole is open. Screw thin wood strips behind the drywall to support the patch, but don't sink the heads of the screws any further than $^1/_{16}$-inch (1mm) below the surface of the drywall or the paper may tear, making the patch more difficult to hide. Once the support structure is in place, cut a patch to fit the opening. Screw the patch to the thin wood strips and tape the joint with the mesh tape. Use a putty knife to apply drywall compound in thin layers $^1/_8$-inch (3mm) over the tape and screw holes. Allow the compound to dry fully before applying the next layer. Last, lightly sand the area to blend the edges of the patch.

Cracks and Visible or Peeling Tape Joints
Tools you'll need: Utility knife, mesh tape, drywall compound, fine-grain sandpaper.

Both situations are handled in the same manner; use a utility knife to cut away the tape or to create an indentation for the mesh tape and drywall compound to adhere. Skipping this step will result in a raised patch. Place the mesh tape over the crack and apply drywall compound in thin layers. Once the compound has dried, sand so the edges are flush with the wall.

Wallpaper and Other Crimes Against Humanity

Renters rejoice—wallpaper removal is not your problem. Most modern wallpaper is simple to remove with a solution of fabric softener and water.

* Amelia Earhart, Jimmy Hoffa, my keys

You can find wallpaper scorers in the home decorating aisle near the paint. Wallpaper scorers cut the surface of the wallpaper without damaging the surface of the Sheetrock beneath it. Once the paper has been scored, spray the surface lightly with fabric softener diluted with warm water. Allow the solution to sit for a few minutes. The paper should peel away or come away from the wall with gentle scraping.** If this technique doesn't work, you can rent a steamer from a hardware store. Follow the directions, and understand that people used to simply wallpaper layer over layer. Removal may be somewhat time intensive. Treat it like an archaeological dig, exploring the tackiness of years gone by. Do not use a metal putty knife on damp Sheetrock. It's too easy to gouge the surface. Instead, use a nylon putty knife or scraper to gently peel away the layers. If the plan is to paint after the wallpaper has been removed, you'll have to wash the wall very well or give it a coat of primer. Tri-sodium phosphate (TSP) is a harsh, but effective cleaner. Always use gloves and rinse the wall carefully. This chemical also roughens the surface of the wall, helping paint more effectively adhere to the surface.

Prime Before You Paint

Always apply drywall compound in thin coats or it may crack. Always use a primer before painting a repair to match the room.

Shoes Are Not Hammers

Hanging shelves and pictures shouldn't end in divorce or community service, but lesser projects have been cited. When hanging art,*** keep in mind that the wall itself, doorways, and other objects will affect whether or not the picture or shelf appears to be straight. Much like possession,

---

** There is a permanent method of wallpaper removal. It involves a match and the accelerant of your choice. Check with your insurance company and local ordinances before attempting.

*** It's not for me to define.

Wall Anchors

Wall anchors simply help you hang objects on walls. Their ratings tell you how much weight the anchor can hold (their load-bearing capacity). The ratings are based on idealistic test conditions and often assume a downward force; do not assume your home's walls meets these standards. A large mirror that leans out from the wall exerts force in a different manner than one that hangs flush. On-site testing is always a best bet.

When choosing an anchor, skip the tiny plastic expansion anchors and go for a threaded anchor or a threaded sleeve, a.k.a. a molly bolt. Note: After you install a threaded sleeve, it isn't easy to remove. If you no longer want to use the anchor, you must countersink it and then patch over the hole.

appearance is nine-tenths of the law. Keep this in mind when hanging pictures. Levels are to be consulted, but they do not have the final say.

When hanging items on a wall, choose a fastener rated for well over the anticipated weight. If a picture weighs 35 pounds, purchase the anchor rated for 50 pounds and understand that it is the anchor and not the drywall that has been rated. Always anchor to a stud when possible and remember wall anchors are designed for walls, not ceilings.

Stud finders are affordable, usually less than twenty dollars, and using one is significantly less time-consuming than filling test holes.

Place a strip of painter's tape on the wall to mark the topmost edge of the frame. The width of the frame should be marked in pencil on the paint strip.

Examine the back side of the frame. Brackets are more precise than wire, but using two hooks can make up for this. If the item is to be hung on a wire, pull the wire taut toward the top of the frame at one or two points, depending on the number of hooks. Measure the distance from the wire to the top of the frame. Mark this distance below the painter's tape, and understand this mark is for the bottom of the hook, not the placement of the fastener. If the item is to be hung on brackets, measure from the bracket to the top of the frame. Additionally, measure where the bracket is widthwise and mark this measurement on the wall.

Drill the hole, then insert the fastener by tapping or screwing it into place, as directed by the instructions. Insert the screw and hook. Hang the picture and make final adjustments as necessary. Masking tape wrapped around a hanging wire can help prevent shifting, and felt furniture pads placed on the back of the lower corners of a frame can prevent wall dings.

In the case of shelving, tracing a paper template can make the job much easier. Shelving should always be anchored in wall studs. Use a stud finder to determine where the placement options are and work within the room's limitations. Tape the template to the wall, ensure it is level—or appears level—and mark the wall through the template for fastener placement. Drill your holes, install the anchors, screw the screws, and hang the shelf.

Hanging Groups of Pictures

When arranging pictures, treat groups of art as one piece. Use newspaper or cardboard to create a template of the arrangement.

Floors

Unlike Raquel Welch, carpet doesn't age gracefully. It wrinkles. And it doesn't matter whether the wrinkles are from improper installation, humidity, or carelessly moving heavy furniture, it all boils down to there being too much carpeting for the room. Carpet wrinkles are trip hazards, but they're easily fixed, and isn't Grandma worth the effort?

Carpet Wrinkles
Tools you'll need: Utility knife, carpet glue.

If a wrinkle is small and out of the main walkway, it can be fixed. At the highest point of the wrinkle, use the utility knife to cut through the carpet backing. Dab a small amount of carpet glue on the bottom side of the carpeting and press flat. Place a heavy object* over the repaired area until the glue has set, then vacuum to hide the repair. If it is a large room with a lot of wrinkles, consider hiring a professional. The rates for tool rental will run about the same as hiring. Plus, the professional then bears the responsibility if a seam separates.

Berber Snags

Tools you'll need: Needle-nose pliers, a small cup of cooking oil, hot glue gun, glue sticks.

Berber carpeting has a tendency to snag and unravel, a lot like a sweater. With a little patience, it isn't difficult to repair a run. Work from the start of the run toward the edge of the carpet. Dip the pliers into the cooking oil** and grasp the loop of carpet just above the first small bit of latex attached to the yarn. Dab a small amount of hot glue onto the backing of the carpet, where the latex was pulled loose. Press the loop into the hot glue and hold until it sets. Repeat until the end of the snag is reached. Allow to set thoroughly before vacuuming.

Burns or Severe Stains

Tools you'll need: Utility knife, tin can (or other template), single-sided carpet tape, painter's tape, pen.

---

* No, deadbeat relatives are not an option.

** Nothing kinky here. The cooking oil is just a release agent to keep the pliers from sticking to the carpet.

If a stain is permanent or the carpeting has been damaged, such as with a burn, a small plug or patch is a useful option. Although a patch is not a perfect fix, it is much less noticeable than a burn or severe stain. Patches or plugs*** are cut from the same carpeting, sometimes from a remnant, but more often from a closet or under a bookshelf that won't be moved. They can still be quite noticeable due to the difference in wear, but this should fade over time.

Place the can over the stained area and use the utility knife to cut through the backing but not the underlying carpet pad. Remove the stained portion of the carpet. Use the same template to cut a matching plug of carpet from an inconspicuous area, preferably from a remnant. Place the plug in the hole, and twist and turn until the least obvious position is found. Use the painter's tape or a sticky note to make marks for alignment on both the plug and the carpet.

Remove the plug from the hole and cut strips of the single-sided carpet tape, slightly longer than the plug. Carefully remove the paper covering the adhesive side of the tape. Tuck the tape, sticky side up, into the hole, anchoring the edges under the edge of the carpet. Once the tape is in place, carefully align the plug with the painter's tape and press into place.

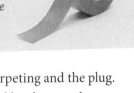

Stabilize With Tape

Covering the area to be cut with painter's tape will stabilize the carpet fibers, giving a cleaner cut.

There will be a slight difference between the old carpeting and the plug. To minimize this effect, place a heavy weight or several books over the patch. Vacuum the area thoroughly after the weight has been removed to further mask the edges of the plug.

*** Much like hair plugs, carpet plugs are a midlife fix for a terminal problem.

Furniture Imprints

Furniture dents are an easy fix, provided the carpet can handle water. Use a wet rag to dampen the dent. While drying the rug with a hair dryer, held about 5 inches (13cm) from the surface, fluff the fibers with a spoon.*

Separated Seams

Tools you'll need: Seaming iron, carpet cutter, hot-melt seam tape, carpet sealer.

Carpet is called wall-to-wall, but in most homes, rooms are wider than a standard roll. To fully carpet a room, installers have to create a seam, which is usually invisible. Sometimes moving furniture or simply poor installation can cause a seam to separate. If it was due to poor installation, contact the company, especially if the flooring is still under warranty. If the carpet is not under warranty, don't worry, it's a relatively painless repair.

For best results, rent a seaming iron and carpet cutter from the hardware store and pick up a roll of hot-melt seam tape and a bottle of carpet sealer. Some low-traffic areas may be fine with one-sided carpet tape, but don't rely on it for busy parts of a home. Use the carpet cutter to finish separating the seam, then carefully dab the sealer on the exposed edges of carpet. This latex agent will help keep tufts of carpeting from coming loose. After the sealant has set, place a strip of the hot-melt seam tape under the edges of the carpet. There are guidelines to help with the proper placement. Remember, the seaming iron does not touch the carpet fiber, rather it sits directly on the glue and is scooted forward a little at a time, as the carpet is pressed into place behind it. Think of the process as zipping the carpet shut. If done properly, the seam shouldn't be noticeable to someone unaware of the repair.** As a home owner, you'll always know and be able to tell. Get over it.

---

   * "Why a spoon, Cousin?" "Because it hurts more!" —*Robin Hood: Prince of Thieves*

 ** If the seam is noticeable, consider limiting your social circle to include only umpires and other sports officials. They have no trouble missing the obvious.

SECTION FOUR
Cook It

SIXTEEN

Burned Water? There's Hope Yet

While most young adults have a metabolism that can handle a diet of pizza and Mountain Dew, there comes a time when broccoli is a welcomed addition, and your colon will thank you. Practice and a willingness to try again are really all it takes to become a competent cook. It's certainly true that not everyone has the desire to be a great cook, but even the least inspired can learn basic techniques to create edible results. If rocking out in the kitchen ranks low on the bucket list, then set a minimum standard, perhaps fourteen meals, that can be used in a rotation. Boring? Possibly, but that and a decent multivitamin should be enough to keep scurvy at bay.

Like swimming,* cooking is a difficult process to learn by theory, but some basic guidelines can give even a discouraged cook some hope.

Mistakes happen. Even great cooks get distracted or have a bad day. Always have a frozen pizza, or P.B. & J. on hand for the night that everything goes wrong. It will happen. Know it going in and never use a special event to practice a new recipe or technique.

---

* "I can swim, I just don't see the point of getting all wet." —Sheldon Cooper

Top Tips for Hopeless Cooks

1. Read the directions all the way through before you start cooking.
2. Use a timer.
3. Preheat.
4. Use all five senses:
   - Taste food before seasoning.
   - If it smells burnt, remove it from the heat.
   - Brown is flavor, black is ruined.
   - Sizzling is good, but popping signals danger, whether by burns or overcooking.
   - Check to see if a pan is hot before adding food. Everyone forgets to turn on a burner now and then.

Invest in Good Equipment

Even a highly experienced cook can be frustrated by flimsy cookware. It's better to have one or two serviceable pots and pans than a cupboard full of useless, thin-bottomed pans that will burn dinner at the drop of a hat. You'll also find food prep much easier with a variety of sharp, quality knives. Chapter 17 covers this topic in more depth.

Find a Trusted Resource

There is a phenomenon referred to as the paradox of choice: After a certain point, having more choices paralyzes consumers as they worry about the drawbacks of choosing one option over another. There are thousands of cookbooks to choose from, and the best option is largely dependent on life-style and personal taste, or lack thereof. When choosing a cookbook, don't be drawn in by fancy pictures; instead, look closely at the ingredients and the directions. Think about the nearest grocery store while paging through the recipes. Do the items look familiar? Are you seeing the same seasonings from one recipe to another? If not, put the book down and try another. These books are usually not intended for normal people.

Some newer editions of classic references have been updated to suit the American reliance on processed food. If a new cook is out to learn technique, a better option is to search for the older versions of classics such as a pre-2000 edition of *The Joy of Cooking* by Irma S. Rombauer. Used bookstores, yard sales, and online searches are great resources.

Cookbooks for the beginner should have clear directions and common ingredients.

Don't be drawn in by gimmick cookbooks. No one needs nine hundred recipes for canned tuna or 365 slow cooker recipes. There may be nine hundred recipes, but the average household would burn out on the idea by recipe ten. Also, stay away from cookbooks written for the latest fad diet, whether it's grapefruits or cabbage soup. The nutrition is suspect and the skills may not necessarily translate to other meals.

Every Meal Doesn't Need to Be an Experiment

This is especially true for families that are used to relying on convenience items. The vast majority of people are suspicious of change. Unless your family already thrives on variety, try not to introduce more than one new flavor a week, and don't abandon successful meals in pursuit of new recipes.*

Real Food Isn't Always Heat-and-Eat

It's easy to get spoiled with the ease of flash-frozen, plastic-wrapped, overly hygienic food. Learning to actually cook sometimes takes getting a little

* "It has raisins in it. You like raisins!" —*Better Off Dead*

messy. Bones and skin provide a depth of flavor processing can't return. Don't worry, most people get a little less squeamish as they become accustomed to dealing with the raw ingredients.

Have a Basic Understanding of Heat

Not all heat transfer is the same. A cook can't switch from one heating method to another without drastically altering the outcome of the dish. This principle is especially true with protein, the major component of meat. Heat causes coagulation, which is a change in the structure of protein. The

Dealing with Picky Eaters

Dear Home-Ec 101,

My husband is hopelessly picky and I see my preschooler is taking after him. Do you have any suggestions on ways I can break the cycle?

Signed,
Short-Order Shirley

You'll be glad to know that requiring normal, healthy kids to eat a varied and healthy diet is not child abuse, despite their loud and obnoxious claims to the contrary.

Most importantly, be the parent, not a short-order cook. Ask for the child's input on one or two meals a week and accommodate if it fits the time, budget, and your ability. Have the child help prepare meals. Even a preschooler can shred lettuce for a salad.

Cook a variety of fresh, whole foods. Can't cook worth a darn? Grab some recipes and start cooking anyway. Cook foods, especially vegetables, in different ways. Just because someone hates steamed asparagus doesn't mean they won't love it broiled. Avoid fast food and takeout. A child's palate becomes accustomed to food engineered to taste good rather than provide nourishment. That's not to say you can never go to these places. Just don't make it the majority of what is served or the kids will learn to hold out for these meals.

Have your kids try foods, even if it's just one bite. And have them try the same foods regularly. Tastes change over time. Young children are particularly sensitive to bitter flavors. This is actually very handy from an evolutionary point of view, as most poisons are bitter. If you get your kids in the habit of at least trying everything, eventually they will start liking new foods.

Finally, take into account your family's likes and dislikes, but don't cater to their every whim. Sure, the kids might love pizza and burgers and chicken nuggets best, but that doesn't mean you have to serve those foods for every meal. If they hate what's for dinner and you don't want them to starve, there's always P.B. & J. (Unless they have a peanut allergy. Then it's just J.)

speed at which coagulation occurs is largely dependent on the type of heat applied. Heat is transferred from the source to food in three distinct manners: conduction, convection, and radiation.

Conduction

Conduction requires contact. Heat is transferred from one item to another, from the pan to the food in the pan. Anytime a pan is used to heat food (whether its warming a can of soup on the stove top or making a grilled cheese sandwich), you are using conduction.

Convection

Convection is heat transfer by the movement of air, water, or oil. Some ovens are specially designed with fans to facilitate the movement of hot air. These ovens are known as convection ovens. Deep-frying is another form of heat transfer by convection, as is boiling, as in the case of cooking pasta.

Radiation

The final contestant on our show today is radiation,* and this is where wave energy moves heat from the source to the food. Microwaves fall under the

A microwave won't heat certain kinds of glass and ceramics, because there's nothing for the waves to interact with. Some cookware gets hot only via conduction; it's actually the food that heats the plate in the microwave.

radiation method of heat transfer. The waves excite water molecules in the food, meaning they vibrate.** The vibration creates friction—which is what actually heats the food. The usual suspect is infrared waves, which are the same waves that cause the shimmer you see on a hot summer day. (And, yes, sunbathing is cooking via radiation.)

* Not the "giant-ants-are-attacking-New-Mexico" kind.
** I said vibrate, not gyrate.

Buy a Meat Thermometer

Just one trip to the ER would pay for a whole slew of twenty-five dollar meat thermometers. Make the investment and never cook a large cut of meat without one. Even well-written recipes can't cover every possible variation when it comes to larger cuts of meat; they all cook at slightly different rates depending on the shape, thickness, starting temperature (some recipes assume meat started at room temperature, when it may have been just pulled from the refrigerator), and oven variations. With all of these factors, cook times are almost always approximations. A meat thermometer takes the variables out of the equation. Splurge a little and get the one with the probe that stays in the roast. The alarm is invaluable for distracted individuals. Shiny!

A Quick Note on Safety

A successful meal won't be remembered if everyone spends the evening in the ER with food poisoning. Luckily there are a few simple ways to avoid that scenario.

Don't Cross Contaminate

Anything that has come in contact with raw meat should be washed and sanitized. This includes counters, cutting boards, knives, and dishtowels. Remember, washing solid surfaces is a two-step process: First use soap, then a disinfecting agent (heat, bleach). The soap gets the bacteria and grime out of tiny crevices.

All produce should be washed before eaten, and if you use reusable grocery bags, give them a wash once in a while, especially if you carry raw meat in them.

Know the Danger Zone

Keep food out of the danger zone. This means all food that isn't "shelf-stable" needs to be kept at 40° F (4° C) or below, and hot foods need to be kept above 140°F (60°C). Any cooked or refrigerated food that lingers between these temperatures should be discarded after two hours.

Wash Your Hands
Wash your hands, before you cook and while you're cooking, if you touch raw meat or eggs or anything that touched raw meat or eggs. Wash your hands if you cough or sneeze. Get friendly with the soap and familiar with clean towels, too.

Watch Your Towels
Dishtowels and washcloths can carry bacteria from one surface to another. If a cloth or towel is used on a potentially contaminated surface, place it in the hamper. Do not get in the habit of using an apron as a handtowel.

SEVENTEEN

Outfit Your Kitchen: Cookware and Small Appliances

Setting up a kitchen can feel overwhelming, and many questions will no doubt worry your mind: What if I buy the wrong thing? What if I spend too much money? How will I ever afford everything I need? Relax. You don't need to purchase everything right away. Bargains can be found at closeout stores, thrift stores, and sometimes factory seconds are a good deal. The most important thing to keep in mind when purchasing an appliance or cookware is the difference between spending money on quality and throwing it away after a trend. There is no need to spend thirty dollars on a bowl for kitchen waste, for instance, when an old ice cream bucket will do. Sure, a plastic ice cream bucket isn't sexy,* but it will probably live under the sink. You should invest a bit more for items you know you will use on a regular basis.

This chapter is a listing of everything you need to fully equip a kitchen that serves a household that eats a majority of meals at home. If you dine out a lot and don't intend to do much cooking, you probably don't need as much equipment. We will tackle kitchenware first, then small appliances.

---

* Check with the glue gun and doily crowd if you actually want ideas for sprucing it up.

Buy the Best

"But the thing was that good boots lasted for years and years. A man who could afford fifty dollars had a pair of boots that'd still be keeping his feet dry in ten years' time, while a poor man who could only afford cheap boots would have spent a hundred dollars on boots in the same time and would still have wet feet."

—The Captain Samuel Vimes' boots theory of socioeconomic unfairness from *Men at Arms* by Terry Pratchett

The quick and dirty list of kitchenware:

1. Pots and pans
2. Knives
3. Mixing bowls
4. Wooden or nylon spoons
5. Spatulas
6. Measuring spoons
7. Measuring cups, both dry and liquid
8. Bakeware (assorted)
9. Baking sheets
10. Broiling pan
11. Vegetable peeler
12. Grater
13. Tongs
14. Cutting boards
15. Whisk
16. Thermometer
17. Can opener (manual)
18. Colander/strainer
19. Utensils, including steak knives
20. Dinnerware and glassware (could be plastic; let's not quibble)

Pots and Pans

Outside of major appliances, a set of pots and pans should be the largest investment in a kitchen. A quality set of cookware, with heavy bottoms, solidly attached ovenproof handles, and tight-fitting lids can make the difference between a miserable cooking experience and a pleasant one. (I prefer glass lids; they make checking items that much easier.) Heavy bottoms distribute heat more evenly than their flimsy counterparts, and I highly recommend stainless steel cookware. Be aware, there is a little bit of a learning curve with stainless, but once a cook gets used to heating a pan before adding the oil or meat, food sticks less and it isn't difficult to clean. A starter set of stainless cookware* is fine for a beginner to moderately skilled cook.

What is a starter set? Usually it's about ten to twelve pieces, including lids. Unless a cook entertains frequently or cooks large meals in bulk, the following pieces are adequate:

- Frying pans, usually two, one small enough for a couple of eggs or a single grilled cheese, and another slightly larger
- A large covered skillet, usually about 12-inches (30cm) in diameter, the lid needs to be tight fitting (no steam vents; stay away from those)
- A casserole, not a ceramic one. This is a pot with two small handles that can be used on the stove or in the oven, like a Dutch oven, but it's usually a little smaller
- A Dutch oven, a sturdy five- to ten-quart pot that is oven safe with a tight-fitting lid
- A stock pot, with a lid and sometimes a basket, which lets the pot double as a steamer

Stainless steel is extremely versatile. It works on electric, gas, smooth top, and inductive ranges.

If your budget is a little more generous, consider supplementing the starter set with enameled cast iron (not suitable for inductive ranges) or,

---

* I use the Emerilware basic set by All-Clad. It has a lifetime warranty. I've used the set for seven years, slowly augmenting with some enameled iron by Le Creuset, which is partly an investment in quality and partly an indulgence in brand snobbery.

Tips for Cooking With Stainless Steel Cookware

- Never use the highest setting on your range, except when boiling water.
- Never use metal utensils.
- When sautéing and pan frying, heat the pan before adding a small amount of oil, tilt the pan to coat the bottom, and then add the food.
- If meat has stuck to the pan during cooking, wait a moment before trying to free it. Sometimes it just needs a little more time. If this doesn't work, use a plastic spatula to free the food.
- If food is stuck to the pan after cooking, fill the pan with water and a little vinegar *or* baking soda. Heat over low to medium heat and allow to simmer for a few moments to loosen food particles. Empty the pan and wash.
- Only certain scouring powders are safe to use with stainless. My favorite is Bar Keepers Friend, which is made from oxalic acid.
- Wash the pots and pans in the dishwasher *only* if the manufacturer suggests it.

if you're lucky enough to have a gas range, plain old-fashioned cast iron. This cookware is quite heavy, but we all could use a little more exercise, right? The slow, even heating is superb, and it is versatile, transferring to the oven (if you purchase a lower-end brand of enameled cast iron, you may need to buy replacement oven-safe knobs for the lids and handles, but these are inexpensive and easy to find online and can save money over the high-end version).

Anodized aluminum is great for large stock pots, an item most beginner cooks can wait to purchase.

Use only wooden, nylon, or silicon utensils with metal cookware. Metal utensils can scratch the surface. When caring for cookware, never use harsh chemicals or metal scouring pads.

Cleaning a Scorched Pan

Dear Home-Ec 101,

Last night, I left an aluminum pot on a burner that I had thought I turned off. I served dinner and by the time I came back to it, all I found was a pan full of burnt food. Is my aluminum pot ruined? How do I remove the mess?

Signed,

Tempted to Toss It Out

Don't worry, your pan is salvageable—it's just going to take some time and elbow grease. Because the pan is aluminum, I do not recommend using the oven cleaner trick that is plastered all over the Internet. The caustic chemicals can etch or chemically scratch the metal, which means almost everything will stick to it in the future.

Fill the pan with enough water to cover the burnt-on food, add some white vinegar, and bring it to a boil. Turn the heat down to low and simmer for twenty minutes. (Try not to forget it this time.)

Pour off the liquid, let the pan cool enough to handle it, and use a nylon scraper or wooden spoon to scrape off as much of the burnt mess as possible. If there is still a lot of burnt food, repeat the process.

Once you've gotten down to the last thin layer, it's time to break out our old pal Bar Keepers Friend, which is an oxalic acid compound and safe for food preparation surfaces. Sprinkle it over the bottom of the pot, which should still be damp, allow it to soak for a few moments, then use a rag and rub with the grain. Rinse the pot well before storing.

If you choose to ignore my advice and go the nonstick route, remember *never* heat an empty nonstick pan, as this may release toxic fumes, which can kill small pets and logically aren't good for humans, either.

Knives

Second only to pots and pans, knives are some of the most important kitchen tools you will own. With knives, it's not about quality as much as it is finding a good fit. It may be generalizing, but most novice cooks haven't discovered their preference for kitchen knives, so don't get lured in by the fancy talk of a salesperson. Don't fall for the knives that "never need sharpening;" they aren't sharp to start with and once dull cannot be sharpened due to their serrated edge.

Avoid carbon steel knives. Yes, they can be sharpened easily, but they lose their edge quickly and discolor some foods, often leaving a metallic taste behind. Stainless steel knives are harder to sharpen but hold an edge for a significantly longer time. The best of the bunch is high-carbon stainless steel; this metal doesn't stain and is more easily sharpened than its stainless steel counterpart. Whichever grade you choose, be sure the knife has a full tang. A tang is the nonsharpened end of the blade. It should run all the way through the handle, giving strength to the entire utensil. Knives without a full tang are prone to breaking and are often of poor quality. Visit a department store or cooking specialty store and ask to handle different knives. Get a feel for the weight and the handle. A poor fit can cause fatigue even for small jobs. If cooking becomes a loved hobby, by all means research and upgrade, but as with photography, the tools don't make the artist. Keep your knives sharp and in good repair. Expect to sharpen them about once a year. Both hardware stores and cooking specialty shops offer this service.

Most households need four knives (outside of steak knives):

French knife/chef's knife: This is the most frequently used knife and the blade size is usually somewhere between 6 to 10 inches (15cm to 25cm). The blade is wider at the heel and tapers to a point. Grasp the blade of the

Seasoning a Pan

Metal pans like stainless and anodized aluminum need to be seasoned before frying eggs. Heat the pan over medium-high heat, add vegetable oil or bacon grease to the pan, swirl to coat evenly, remove from the heat, and wipe out with a paper towel. Allow the pan to cool completely before using. Pans will need to be reseasoned after washing, but can be scrubbed out with salt to clean between eggs.

knife between the thumb and the forefinger of your dominant hand. The other fingers should be curled loosely around the handle.

Utility knife or boning knife: These two knives are quite similar and most novice cooks need only one or the other. The blade on a utility (or salad knife) is from 6 to 8 inches (15cm to 20cm), while a boning knife is slightly thinner and is usually 6 inches (15cm) in length. This can double as a carving knife for cooked meats. When picking out your first set, go with the most comfortable handle. The knives are somewhat interchangeable at this skill level. Just be sure to get a knife with a stiff blade, rather than a flexible one meant to filet only fish and other delicate items. The proper grip for this knife is similar to that for the chef's knife, but only around the handle, not the blade itself.

Paring knives: A paring knife is great for coring and peeling fruit whose skin is too thick for a vegetable peeler. This shorter knife has a blade from 2 to 4 inches (5cm to 10cm) in length. The grip may be different for certain jobs, but it is usually held in the curve of the four fingers of the dominant hand; the index and middle finger guide the blade with the ring and pinky finger stabilizing the handle. The user cuts toward the thumb in a slow, controlled manner.

Serrated knife: This knife has a long blade that is serrated (surprise!). It's good for cutting breads and cakes.

Other Utensils

The rest of the equipment on this list doesn't require a huge investment (at least not until we get to small appliances).

Mixing bowls. Stainless and glass are both good choices for mixing bowls. Plastic works most of the time, but it will scratch and it needs to be cleaned more carefully because over time grease will work its way into those scratches.

Wooden spoons. With a little food-grade mineral oil, wooden spoons can last a while, but most of the time I just grab a small pack of the cheapest variety and replace as needed. Having several around eliminates the temptation to reach for metal spoons, which can scratch the cooking surface of many pots and pans. Wooden spatulas are great for preventing scorching, as they have a nice flat surface to scrape food from the bottom of a pan. If you hate the feel of wood, nylon makes a great alternative—just don't place it on a hot burner. Melted plastic is never fun.

Spatulas. I use three kinds of spatulas: rubber for scraping, slotted nylon for removing pan fried items from oil, and regular nylon (stiff) for lifting heavier items.

Measuring spoons. I typically eyeball most recipes, but there are times where accurate measurements are a must. I prefer sizes $1/8$ teaspoon to 1 tablespoon metal spoons on a single ring. Ring or not, the spoons will disappear over time if there are roommates, spouses, or gremlins about. Be prepared to replace these every few years and after each move. Oval spoons often fit into spice containers a little easier, but don't buy the gimmick adjustable ones. They are difficult to clean. Plus, there's only one to lose and it will get lost.

Measuring cups. For dry ingredients, you'll need sizes $1/8$ cup to 1 cup. They are available in metal or plastic. The metal ones seem to be a little easier to clean and don't have to be peeled off of the heating element in the bottom of the dishwasher. Like the wandering measuring spoons, measuring cups seem to get lost with a logic-defying regularity, so don't spend a lot on them.

I have two liquid measuring cups, a 1-cup size and a 4-cup size. Both are glass. Don't bother with the plastic versions because their markings fade if washed in the dishwasher.

Bakeware. The box sets are perfectly fine. If you choose metal, be sure to look for all aluminum as opposed to coated steel. Metal bakeware gets dinged and bent. Ceramic and glass versions crack or break. Don't go nuts, but a big family may need a second set. While you're at the store, don't forget a couple of 8- or 9-inch (20cm–23cm) square or round cake pans.

Baking or cookie sheets. Keep three to five baking sheets on hand. They are useful for a lot more than just baking cookies. Replace these as they become rusted or warped. Many cities have restaurant supply stores that are open to the public and often have quality sheet pans at a decent price. Some people shop for shoes, I look at restaurant-grade equipment and drool.*

Broiling pan. These are often included with an oven, but apartment dwellers may find theirs have wandered off. They come in handy for broiling (naturally), oven frying, and even for letting the fat drip away from meat loaf.

Vegetable peeler. Skip the one with the plain metal handle and find one that is comfortable. Don't spend a lot because it will need to be replaced when the blade dulls.

Grater. I have three graters in different sizes that were sold as a pack for less than five dollars. You can also go with a box grater. Either way works.

Tongs. Tongs are a must. They come in handy for turning food as well as steadying some meats while carving. Generally, I prefer the pinch-style tongs instead of the scissor-style tongs, but in either case, silicon tips make the world a better place.

Cutting boards. Vegetarians can get by with one or two. Omnivores need three: two for fruits, vegetables, and cooked meat, and a separate one for raw meat. Be sure to sanitize them after use. Wash with dish detergent, then use diluted chlorine bleach (at 200 parts per million): 1 tablespoon bleach per gallon of water (4ml per 4L).

* Tiffany's versus Williams Sonoma? Pfft, no contest there.

Whisk. I've found a difference between the name-brand and off-brand silicon-coated whisks. The off-brand wires bend easily, and their silicon coating shreds quickly. So it's worth buying the name-brand whisk. Have a least one silicon-coated whisk for stirring hot items without scratching a pan. A plain metal whisk is fine for beating eggs.

Thermometer. Thermometers are invaluable, and a quality one can be had for about twenty-five bucks. I prefer the electronic type with the probe that can be left in the meat and a cord that attaches to a unit outside of the oven. This eliminates the need to open the oven door to check the temperature (which lets out heat and moisture). If you have a lot of interest in making sweets and desserts, go ahead and buy a candy thermometer, too.

Can opener. Unless canned food is a significant portion of your diet or arthritis is an issue, a manual (versus electric) can opener is sufficient. It's cheaper, smaller, and you'll be everyone's friend during a power outage. As a bonus, most double as a bottle opener.

Strainer/colander. You don't need a pasta pot. This bowl with holes isn't nearly as complicated as the commercials want you to believe. A strainer is not a high-end kitchen item. If you want a fancy, colored enameled strainer, that's your deal. Just avoid the thin, plastic ones. It's far too easy to accidentally melt a plastic colander by absent-mindedly setting it on a hot burner.

Utensils, dishes, and glassware (oh my!). Utensils, dishes, and glassware are completely up to the individual. Just watch for lead warnings and be aware that not all finishes are dishwasher safe. When purchasing dishes, be sure to be able to accommodate the occasional guest. Plastic cutlery and paper plates work for occasional informal entertaining,

Nice Extras to Have

These last couple I don't consider a necessity, but they are certainly nice to have on hand:

Pastry cutter. Look for fine blades rather than wires. They are also great for mashing potatoes.

Garlic press. If your knife skills aren't up to par, this makes mincing garlic a breeze, but it's kind of a pain to clean.

Wine tool. These are handier than a plain corkscrew for opening wine bottles and fold compactly like a pocketknife.

Rolling pin. In addition to rolling out the occasional piecrust, I use mine to pound chicken breasts and crush crackers, walnuts or pecans, but a novice cook can get by with a wine bottle for these tasks, if they happen only occasionally. It also has the added benefit as a weapon in case of zombie apocalypse.

The Great Small Appliance Rundown

Space is a priority in many kitchens and your small appliances need to be chosen carefully with budget and space as the top considerations. The best small appliances are those that are either used daily or have multiple uses.

Microwave. Even noncooks get this. As a proficient cook, I use it frequently to reheat leftovers, and heat liquids to add to recipes. I rarely use mine for actual cooking.

Mixer. A serious baker will want a stand mixer, but someone who only occasionally whips up a batch of muffins will fare well with a handheld version or simply spoons.

Blenders and immersion blenders. Soup and smoothie fans can certainly justify a blender. For those who dig mixed drinks, a standard blender is a must. Most stick blenders don't crush ice, but they make pureeing soup a snap.

Toasters and toaster ovens. Singles and couples may want to consider a toaster oven over a traditional slotted toaster. This can be energy saving for small entrees or for melting cheese on sandwiches, rather than turning on the large oven. Large families may find it just as efficient to broil a sheet pan of bread at one time.

Coffee pots and electric kettles. Caffeine fiends and tea aficionados will agree: either or both of these are a must-have. Some coffee drinkers use a nonelectric French press, but this is usually only worthwhile if you have a coffee grinder, as the nuance of the effort would be lost with preground.

Slow cookers. The name Crock-Pot is broadly applied, but it is a trademarked name that only applies to a single brand of slow cookers. Before delving into Grandma's slow cooker recipe book, be aware that, due to safety codes, newer models cook much faster than the previous generation did. Be prepared: a recipe that suggests six to eight hours may be ready in four.

Vegetable steamer. Round out any meal with steamed fresh or frozen vegetables, season and serve. Many also double as rice cookers.

Rice cookers. If rice is a common staple at dinner, a rice cooker can be a handy appliance. Personally, I use a pot with a tight fitting lid.

Electric griddles and indoor grills. These related appliances are exceptionally useful for singles or large families. Singles, especially apartment dwellers, may like small indoor electric grills for the convenience. Indoor grills will never compete with a true grill, but for speed and ease they can't be beat. Large electric griddles, on the other hand, offer great value in their expansive cooking surface, which makes cooking pancakes, fried eggs, or other items for a crowd a less time-consuming process.

Not all of these appliances are right for every household. Before making a purchase, understand that no single appliance will revolutionize your aptitude for cooking. Having the proper tools can help, but it is practice and perseverance that make a cook, not a fancy juicer purchased on a whim.

EIGHTEEN

Recipe Rundown: Deciphering Terms and Basic Techniques

Why should someone learn to cook in the first place? What is the point when there are so many convenience foods readily available? I can't answer for others, but I can tell you why I cook from scratch; I want to know exactly what is used in my food. I want to use real, fresh ingredients. If I make it myself, my goal is nutrition and taste, not profit and shelflife. I am also teaching my children to cook. By doing so I am ensuring their palates are accustomed to real food, not food engineered to feel and taste good. Yes, there is a difference between store-bought and homemade, and if possible, I want my kids to crave the foods that are closest to the real deal.

With a little common sense, cooking from scratch can be healthier. Pediatric kidney stones are on the rise in the United States. The cause? Excess salt. This salt not only comes from the expected sources—chips and french fries—but also processed foods such as sandwich meats and canned soups. Those prepacked lunches in the dairy case have an absurd amount of sodium. Sports drinks designed to rehydrate athletes are loaded with salt.* There's no need for a child to become accustomed to consuming these products.

* Electrolytes have their place, but channel surfing is not an endurance sport.

It's best not to make consuming flavor enhancers like monosodium glutamate (MSG) a habit. MSG works a lot like salt, making food taste better, but it's like salt on steroids** and it can make even food of very poor quality taste fantastic. If the human palate adjusts to this level of stimulation, regular food can seem bland by comparison.

Finally, cooking from scratch often produces less waste than convenience food, which is way overpackaged. I don't want to be preachy (it's too late, I know), but convenience foods have a cost. My goal, when I started the website Home-Ec101.com, was to help our readers learn the alternatives so they have a choice when it comes to feeding themselves and their families.

I didn't learn to cook until I was an adult. My initiation to cooking was a trial-by-fire week when my boss decided to leave town and I had to fill his shoes as a cook in the restaurant where I was working. I had been lurking around the kitchen looking over his shoulder for a while, and that week inspired a love of cooking. A couple of years later I worked my way through the line at a very nice steakhouse in Minnesota. I started in prep, cutting bread, slicing 50-pound bags of onions, dicing tomatoes and fruit by the bucket. As new cooks were hired and others promoted, I slowly moved up the line through salads to fry to broiler (that was the grill) to flat top and expeditor. I had just started with saute when a complicated pregnancy ended my restaurant career.

Cooking for a family is different. Yes, I learned a lot of skills that helped me make the transition, but cooking with kids underfoot and on a budget is a far cry from having the best and freshest ingredients on hand on someone else's dime.***

You don't have to have experience working in the food industry to become a cook. I once had a chemistry teacher who assured us that if we could bake a cake, chem labs would be easy as pie and vice versa.

** Mrs. Paul and the Gorton's Fisherman are being brought before Congressional hearings.

*** Or someone else's Benjamin, when truffle butter is involved.

If you are a new cook, focus on being methodical—follow recipes and compare the results with your expectations. Keep a notebook, a journal, or a blog (I hear those are popular now) of your experiments. Turn failures into learning experiences. What was it you or your family hated about a recipe? Was it the raisins in the curry of the mayonnaise in the spaghetti, or perhaps that was just one too many exotic ingredients for their Hamburger Helper palates?

The difference between cooking a simple recipe and the boxed meal is the proximity of the ingredients at the start of the process.

Read the Entire Recipe

Anytime time you plan to do some cooking, start by reading the entire recipe from start to finish. After you read the recipe once, read it again, just for good measure.

Sometimes the author of a recipe may leave an ingredient out of the list but include it in the instructions. Sometimes this isn't a problem, but what if a critical ingredient didn't make it to the shopping list? Don't get taken by surprise.

Know the Ingredients

Look over the ingredient list and get a general feel for the role each ingredient plays. For instance, in many gravies there will be a fat, flour (or sometimes corn starch, but we can fight about that later), and a liquid. The fat plays a role in flavor delivery and binds with the flour to thicken the liquid.

If a dish includes rice or pasta, you'll need water or some form of liquid such as stock or broth. Rice dishes will always have at least a 2:1 liquid to rice ratio. If the liquid doesn't arrive in the form of water or broth, maybe the recipe assumes the liquid will come from canned tomatoes or beans. In that case, you don't want to drain the tomatoes or beans before adding them to the dish.

Incredible Eggs

Eggs do a lot of work in the kitchen. In baked goods they give structure. Egg yolks help make batters smooth. When creamed with butter and sugar, they incorporate air into the batter, making baked goods less dense, and they bring a lot of moisture to a recipe.

When beating egg whites, start with room temperature eggs to get the most volume. Start slow and gradually increase the speed. If the egg whites are to be incorporated into a batter, gently fold them in. Slide the spatula down the side of the bowl, pull to the center, and repeat, turning the bowl just until the eggs are distributed evenly. Too much work will pop the bubbles.

With meringues, it is important to have the oven preheated and bake immediately. Time is the enemy.

If you substitute bouillon cubes for homemade stock, you need to eliminate any additional salt or run the risk of a very salty dish.

Acidic items like tomatoes, lemon juice, or buttermilk often play a larger role than the flavor they provide. In baked goods, the acidic ingredient drives the chemical reaction that causes quick breads and cookies to rise. Sometimes acidity preserves color, and with meats, it is often used to break down proteins and increase tenderness.

Take Inventory, Are All Ingredients on Hand?

Become familiar with the *mise en place* routine. Don't panic; if you've ever watched a cooking show, you've seen this in action. *Mise en place* means the ingredients are all lined up, measured, and ready to go. This task may seem like OCD overkill (and in a way it is), but the act of premeasuring the ingredients forces new cooks to go over their lists one last time. Plus, you may know you have sugar in the cupboard, but how much do you have left? It's better to find out that you're ¼ cup short before you start mixing everything together.

Do You Have the Tools Needed?

Is the kitchen equipment up to the job? There's nothing quite like making a three-layer cake and discovering there are only two 8-inch (20cm) pans in the house.

But don't worry, not all fancy tools are necessary. See the sidebar on the next page for an idea of what you can substitute. But don't get carried away. Old pantyhose may be great for storing onions, but I wouldn't use your old fishnet stockings in place of cheesecloth.

If a recipe calls for parchment paper, waxed paper is not always a decent substitute. It will work if you're chilling an item, but you shouldn't put waxed paper in the oven. A wooden spoon or whisk can be used in place of a mixer, but before starting, take a look at the mixing time. Is your stirring arm up to the task at hand? Whipping egg whites to a stiff peak by hand takes a significant amount of work.

Don't assume that one appliance can stand in for another. Microwaving a steak is not the same as grilling, and broiling is not quite the same as baking.

"It's only two egg whites . . . How hard can it be?"
—Mr. Solos, two hours before slathering his arm in Tiger Balm.

Understand the Terms Used in the Directions

Are all of the cooking terms in the recipe familiar? If not, do some research. Unfamiliar terms don't necessarily equal a complicated or difficult process. A basic explanation may be all you need to set you on your way. Here are quick definitions of some of the most common cooking terms.

Al Dente: This term is used with pasta and some vegetables; it literally means "to the tooth." Al dente generally implies firm but not mushy.

Au Gratin:* The dish has a browned or crusted top, usually with cheese, bread crumbs, and a rich sauce.

---

* Or all rotten, in my house.

Substitute Kitchen Equipment

Does your recipe call for weights or some other gizmo you don't have? Here are some quick substitution ideas:

- **Food weight or bacon press:** Use a foil-wrapped brick. The purpose of the weight is to keep the food in contact with the cooking surface rather than shrinking and curling, in the case of bacon, or contracting, in the case of a half chicken.
- **Cruets:** These are fancy jars for salad dressing. Any clean jar with a tight lid will do.
- **Rolling pin:** Use a wine bottle.
- **Pie weights:** Use dried beans.
- **Pastry blender:** This tool is used to cut butter into flour; two forks can do the job with just a bit more perseverance.

Bake: To cook foods by surrounding them with hot, dry air as in an oven. It's very similar to *roast*, but in general refers to breads, pastries, vegetables, and fish.

Batter: A semiliquid mixture used while making cakes or breads *or* for coating an object to be deep fried.

Boil: To cook in water (or another liquid) rapidly bubbling at 212˚ F (100˚ C).

Braise: To cook in a covered pot or pan with a small amount of liquid. If the dish is meat-based, it is often browned first. This is not the case with vegetables.

Butterflied: Cut partially open, usually so the food will lay flat or to increase the surface area.

Carmelization/Carmelized: Browning or browned sugars caused by heat. This method is often used with sweet onions.

Chop: To cut into irregular pieces.

Convection Oven: An oven in which the hot air is circulated by a fan. Not all home ovens are convection. Using the convection feature will decrease the cooking time, but use care if a recipe does not specify the use of a convection oven.

Creaming: If a recipe says to cream butter and sugar with eggs, this is to incorporate air into the batter by mixing the ingredients together until they are fluffy. Don't shortcut this step.

Dash: A small amount, usually somewhere between $\frac{1}{16}$ and $\frac{1}{8}$ of a teaspoon.

Deglaze: To swirl or stir a liquid into a pan to dissolve cooked food particles or particles on the bottom of the pan. This technique greatly increases the flavor of many sauces and gravies.

Emulsion: A uniform mixture of two unmixable liquids, such as oil and water. Salad dressings are frequently emulsions.

Herbs: The leaves of certain plants used in flavoring.

Marinate: To soak a food in a seasoned liquid.

Mince: To chop into very fine pieces.

Parboil: To partially cook in boiling or simmering water.

Pinch: Half the amount of a dash, usually between $\frac{1}{32}$ and $\frac{1}{16}$ teaspoon.

Poach: To cook gently in water or another liquid that is hot, but not actually bubbling, from 160°F to 180°F (71°C to 82°C).

Reduce: To cook by simmering until the quantity is reduced, thereby concentrating flavors.

Consider the Costs

If a recipe uses seasonings that are not normally stocked, it can significantly increase the perceived cost of the dish. Assuming the spice will be used in other meals, estimate the portion used, rather than the cost of the entire bottle. If it is unknown whether or not anyone likes the flavor, some spice companies offer sample sizes perfect for trying in one or two recipes.

Roast: To cook foods by surrounding with hot, dry air, usually referring to meat.

Saute: To cook quickly in a small amount of fat, such as butter or oil.

Sear: To brown the surface of a food quickly at a high temperature. This does not seal in the juices of meat, but it does create flavor.

Spice: Any part of a plant other than the leaves used to flavor foods.

Sweat: To cook in a small amount of fat over low heat, usually covered.

Temper: To raise the temperature of a cold liquid gradually by stirring in a hot liquid. Eggs are often tempered when added to sauces to avoid scrambling.

Zest: The colored part of the peel of citrus fruits.

Don't Underestimate the Importance of Knife Skills

Just like getting to Carnegie Hall, it takes practice to rock in the kitchen. Always use a cutting board. Scarred countertops are bacterial stomping grounds, so why lay out the welcome mat? Terms like slicing, dicing, and mincing all have specific meanings when they are used in a recipe.

Slicing

If a recipe uses the term *slicing*, typically it will follow up with an estimated size of the slice, ⅛-inch (3mm), ½-inch (13mm), and so on. Don't break out the ruler; estimating is perfectly fine. When slicing long vegetables, such as celery or carrots, do not lift the tip of the knife from the cutting board. Use

Boil Vs. Simmer

Dear Home-Ec 101,

I'm embarrassed to actually ask this, but what is the difference between boiling and simmering? A lot of your recipes say "bring to a boil and reduce the heat to a simmer." What does that mean and why does it matter?

Signed,
Steeped in Stockholm

High school chemistry flashback: Water is made up of molecules of two hydrogen atoms and one oxygen atom. When these molecules are at a temperature between 33˚ F (0.5˚ C) and 211˚ F (99˚ C), they are in a liquid form (known as water). Below 32˚ F (0˚ C), the molecules become a solid (known as ice). When the molecules are above 212˚ F (100˚ C), they become a gas (known as steam).

The bubbles you see rising to the surface of boiling water is the gas form of the molecules escaping from the liquid form of the molecules. The surface tension of water molecules (their tendency to stick together) is what gives the bubbles their round shape. When a bubble reaches the top of the water, it bursts and the steam escapes into the air.

Once the boiling point is reached, even if you turn up the burner, the liquid will not increase in temperature. It may boil more vigorously as more liquid turns into gas, but it won't get any hotter. Most of the time, recipes will call for a liquid to be

your free hand to hold the vegetable stable and guide the vegetable with your fingertips. The professional technique has the side of the blade actually touching the knuckles, but honestly, I've never found a comfortable rhythm with this method. Rock the blade through the vegetable and make slices as uniform as possible. A uniform thickness ensures the pieces all cook at the same rate. For cold foods, it gives the dish a more pleasing appearance.

brought to a boil first. This is to compensate for the drop in temperature that will occur when food is added to the cooking liquid.

The boiling point is too hot for cooking many foods; some starches like pasta and certain vegetables are the exception.

Simmering is the stage before the bubbles have enough energy to break the surface tension. The temperature range for simmering is from 185° F–205° F (85° C–96° C). Not only does simmering require less energy from your appliance, it also keeps many proteins from becoming tough. This is why soups and stews are simmered rather than boiled. The vigorous bubbling action of boiling can break apart some items, including fish.

Most of the time, slow cookers are designed to cook in the simmering range, but you should test out your appliance by filling it partway with water and allowing it to reach temperature at both the high and low settings before leaving an item unattended for an extended period of time. Not all stoves or ranges make simmering easy. In fact, simmering on some gas stoves can be quite difficult. It may be necessary to position the pot so it is not centered over the flame. Be careful to ensure the pot is still balanced and won't tip easily.

Last tidbit, sometimes menus at restaurants will refer to meat as boiled. It's not, it's just an inaccurate description.

Chopping

When a recipe says to chop an item, it means your cut pieces should be of roughly the same size, but the exact shape doesn't matter. Herbs such as parsley and cilantro are often roughly chopped, as are vegetables of uneven textures, like broccoli* and cauliflower. Gather the washed herbs in a pile.

* "And my lady, she went downtown, she bought some broccoli, she brought it home, she's choppin' broccoli. Choppin' brocco-li. Choppin' brocco-laa-aa." –Dana Carvey

The tip of the knife should remain in contact with the cutting board, and the blade should be rocked through the pile. Occasionally, gather the herbs or vegetables back together and work through. Terms such as *coarse* and *rough* imply that the pieces should be uneven, that a variety of texture is expected.

Dicing

In contrast to chopping, dicing is a precise term. Diced vegetables are expected to be of uniform size and shape. This is to ensure even cooking and uniform texture. As onions are like ogres,* there's a special technique to getting an even dice. Cut off the tip (this is the opposite of the root end). Slice the onion in half, pole to pole, not through the equator. Peel off the papery layers and place cut-side down on the cutting board. With the knife parallel to the cutting board, cut from the tip toward the root about ¼ inch (6mm) from the cutting board, while holding the vegetable steady with the fingertips of the guiding hand, do *not* cut all the way through to the root. Repeat this two or three more times depending on the size of the onion. Next, insert the tip of the knife near, but not through the root, and cut even slices from the root to the cut end. Use the tips of your thumb and smallest finger to hold the onion together, with the tips of the other fingers keeping the onion steady. Start from the cut end and make even slices at a right angle to the last set you cut. The onion will fall into a nice, even dice. The first few times you try this method you will be quite slow. Understand that speed comes only with practice.

What About Halving and Doubling Recipes?

Some websites, such as AllRecipes.com, make it very easy to halve or double recipes with just the click of a button. After all, it's just a matter of multiplying fractions, right? Any computer can do it.

---

* According to Shrek they have layers.

Don't Adjust the Temperature

Increasing the oven temperature is not a shortcut. This leads to burnt outsides and raw centers. Patience, Daniel-san.

There is a problem, however: These recipes usually haven't been thoroughly tested. While they turn out well for the given ratios, the recipe may contain errors. These errors aren't usually noticeable until they are amplified. One example is if a regular recipe has slightly too little liquid; the liquid shortfall will be greater if the recipe is doubled. Before you double a recipe, first make it as written to test it out. After you are familiar with the entire process, you should be able to detect any differences in the dish as you prepare a doubled batch.

Adjust Cooking Times

Doubling a recipe also may change the cook time. The length of time a recipe needs to cook depends more on surface area than on the actual volume or weight. Two chickens put in the oven at the same time will finish at the same rate as a single chicken. But, a casserole doubled and simply placed in a larger pan will take longer to cook, as the volume increased more than the surface area. If the doubled recipe is portioned into two pans that are the size called for in the original recipe, the cook time will be unchanged from the original.

If a recipe designed for a skillet is placed in a large stockpot or Dutch oven, it may take longer to cook, because the food's contact with the heat source, in this case the bottom of the pan, is reduced. In some cases there may not be enough evaporation, causing foods to steam instead of sauté.

The moral of the story is: give yourself extra time when doubling recipes. Start with the original cook time and check the dish every five or ten minutes depending on its appearance at the end of the original cook time.

Halving a recipe may significantly decrease the cook time of a recipe. Proportionally, a halved recipe has more surface area exposed to the heat source and will cook in a shorter length of time.

New Cook's Recipe for Successful Entertaining

Don't make a recipe you aren't familiar with when serving guests. Try new recipes when there is no pressure, take notes, and as your experience grows, so will your confidence in trusting your experience and your instinct. Into everyone's lives a little entertaining must fall. Suck it up and make the best of it.

Holiday Menu Planning

When cooking for a crowd, you need to know how many people are dining and have a rough idea of their usual appetite. The list below accounts for serving sizes for average people. If you are serving teenagers or relatives that you already know are greedy eaters, increase the estimates. I increase the dessert estimate just because it's a holiday for Pete's sake. These estimates work best for a formal meal where everyone sits down and eventually people get tired of passing items. If you're serving buffet style, definitely increase the gravy. I don't know what it is about a buffet, but it makes people dig gravy.

- Whole turkey:* 1 pound (453g) of turkey for each guest up to a 14-pound (6.4kg) bird. Anything larger, estimate ¾-pound (340g) per person. (The skeleton of the turkey weighs less proportionally in large birds).
- Bone-in turkey breast: ⅔ pound (304g) per person
- Boneless turkey breast: ½ pound (227g) per person
- Dressing: ¾ cup per guest
- Gravy: ⅓ cup per person

* If you love leftovers, as I do, increase your turkey estimate by 50 percent.

Coordinate Cooking Times

Dear Home-Ec 101,

How can I get better about getting everything on the dinner table at the same time? When I cook for company, the potatoes are raw, the roast is overdone, and the pie is soggy.

Signed,
Scattered Skye

The short answer is, new cooks have to put more thought into planning a meal. When cooking for company, it's easy to be distracted by a desire to impress. New cooks often select several recipes that require a lot of work at the same time, usually just before serving.

Instead, try planning a meal where preparation can be done in stages. Rather than having three items that require the oven at different temperatures, consider having a cold item as a side, such as potato or pasta salad. Frequently these items can be prepared the night before an event, reducing the amount of stress placed on the cook.

Roasts and whole poultry require standing time, usually about thirty minutes prior to serving. Use this to your advantage. Items such as roasted broccoli or simple casseroles can be popped into the oven to cook while the main item rests. Remember these quick-cooking items should be prepped while the roast or chicken is cooking. Always assume items will take longer to prepare if there is a special occasion, extended family, or alcohol involved.

Also consider serving pastas with lots of vegetables so you don't need to prepare additional side dishes. Serve with a salad and there's really no coordination required.

For dessert, always use a timer and never assume you'll remember to pull a pie out of the oven halfway through dinner. Better yet, when the guests ask what they can bring, suggest dessert and pass on the responsibility altogether.

- Mashed potatoes: 1 pound (453g) of potatoes for every three guests
- If serving two kinds of potatoes (roasted and mashed), estimate 1 pound (453g) for every four guests
- Cranberry relish/sauce: 1 pound (453g) of berries for every five people
- Vegetables, including sweet potatoes: ½ cup per person of each type.
- Dessert: one to two servings per guest.

Some of the very dedicated choose to serve both turkey and ham. In that case, estimate 1 pound (453g) of ham for every four or five people and ¾ pounds (340g) of turkey.

Helping Hands

Often when entertaining, one or two guests will insist they would like to help. Prepare for this by having the recipes printed and posted where they can be referenced by anyone. If it's a large meal, create a schedule with the times that dishes need to be started and completed. Set serving dishes out well in advance of needing them, and if it's a large meal, place a notecard with the name of the recipe that will be served in that dish. This helps eliminate questions that may distract you while you're measuring.

Cheaters Don't Always Get Caught

Fancy grocery stores and caterers were invented to help important meals go smoothly, right? Visit well in advance of your event to get ideas. Check out the meat department for prestuffed pork chops or other fancy cuts that simply need to be baked. The deli almost always has a selection of pasta dishes and salads. Don't be afraid to ask for samples. Look in the display window, does the food look appetizing? If it doesn't look great in the store, it's not going to look great the night of your party.

Be sure to ask if the menu changes frequently; you don't want to plan the meal and then discover your dish isn't available on that day. Place your order early if necessary.

Be human. In most cases guests are perfectly understanding if you call in a little help, but if you just can't live with the idea, bring the food home and assemble it in your own serving dishes. Just be sure the hot food is piping hot. If you plan on passing it off as your own, you need to have a recipe or a good excuse as to why you can't share—someone will always ask. Finally, dispose of all of the packaging before the guests arrive.

NINETEEN

Pantry Principles: Are You Ready for the Zombie Apocalypse?

What Exactly Is a Pantry?

By definition, a pantry is a room outside of the kitchen where dry goods are stored. I tend to take a broader view. For some people, the pantry is a few shelves in the kitchen; for others it's an empty linen closet. (How can you manage to empty that closet? Easy, store the spare sheets flat between the mattress and box spring of each bed.*) Still others take advantage of the space under beds or in a basement to store food for a rainy day. Any dry place is a candidate for food storage.

A deep freeze also is an integral part of a well-stocked pantry in North American homes. Craigslist and Freecycle are two fantastic resources for procuring an inexpensive freezer, especially in military towns. Even apartment dwellers can find a space for a small chest freezer. Sure it's not the most attractive end table, but where food is involved, I'm a function-over-form kind of girl.

A well-stocked pantry means you will have a reasonable rotation of

---

* Or between the mattress and floor if you still decorate in "my first apartment" motif. Some people never move past this stage.

ingredients from which to meal plan. You'll also have a stock of food for emergencies—whether they're personal, financial, or weather related.

The Nonemergency Pantry

What do you cook? If the answer is not much, then canned soups, chili, spaghetti sauce, and pasta will probably take up the most space in your pantry. Having a few frozen meals on hand is good, too. A stash of sports-drink powder, your favorite hot beverage ingredients, saltines, and frozen juice concentrate is useful for when the stomach flu hits and you're too sick to venture out.

For the rest of you, take a look at the fall-back meals, that is, what is thrown together when no one wants to cook but there is no money for takeout? Do you make pancakes for dinner? Then make sure there is always flour, sugar, baking powder, salt, and syrup on hand, or a box of complete pancake mix. This is the start of your pantry.

Next, ask yourself, when you cook, what ingredients do you reach for most often? Canned tomatoes? Canned beans? Start purchasing an extra can or two on each trip to the store.

What frozen vegetables will everyone eat? Sure, fresh and local are best, but frozen is a close second while canned is certainly better than no vegetables at all.

Keep powdered nonfat milk on hand for cooking. While some families swear their kids will drink it, I can't get over the taste, but I can still use it in a cooked food like macaroni and cheese. Plus, you can fall back on the powdered milk if you are in a pinch and no one wants to make a last-minute dash to the store.

Rotate the Stock

When unloading the grocery haul, rotate your stock by bringing the oldest to the front and placing the newest in the back.

Pantry Staples

Dear Home-Ec 101,

My son will be moving* into an apartment and setting up a kitchen for the first time. What would be a good basic list of food staples (salt, pepper, sugar, canola oil) to set him up with?

Signed,

Not Mother Hubbard

*While not rocket science,** setting up a pantry is very dependent upon personal tastes and habits. The lists below are by no means all inclusive. If your son's diet leans toward a certain ethnicity, be sure to include the common seasonings or ingredients.*

Basic Pantry Staples:

- *cooking spray, vegetable oil, olive oil*
- *brown and white sugar*
- *plain flour*
- *baking powder and baking soda*
- *pasta*
- *rice*
- *canned tomatoes: diced, pureed, sauce, and paste*
- *canned beans*
- *rolled oats*
- *vinegar*
- *peanut butter*
- *corn starch*
- *cocoa powder*
- *Alka Seltzer****

---

* Yea, more basement space!

** It may not be rocket science but it is "family and consumer science," the modern term for home economics.

*** Useful after playing guess-the-expiration-date.

Make sure the flour and sugar are stored in airtight containers. Young adults are not always the best about observing use-by dates. Consider adding to this list bouillon, soup base, or canned/boxed stock.

Basic Spice Rack:
- black pepper
- basil
- oregano
- thyme
- chili powder
- cumin
- cinnamon
- Italian seasoning

If he likes to broil or grill meats, consider adding some premixed rubs for variety.

Stocking the fridge:
- ketchup
- mustard
- mayonnaise or Miracle Whip
- salad dressing
- jams or jellies
- butter
- shortening or refined coconut oil
- cheese

A three-ring binder with recipes for his favorite meals would be a nice touch. You certainly don't have to be fancy, but page protectors are always helpful. Don't worry that he won't come home for those meals if he can make them himself. No matter how well you transcribe the recipe, it'll never be "just the way Mom used to make."

The Pantry Principle

Stock Up on Sales

If you are looking to stock your pantry for the first time, look for loss leaders. Grocery stores operate with a loss leader rotation.

With practice and patience, it's not too difficult to learn when your staples will be on sale. With a little trial and error, a shopper can learn to buy just enough of the staple to last until the next sales cycle. Sure, occasionally you'll look like the crazy cat lady with a cart full of tuna,* but that doesn't matter. It will be there when it is needed.

Rotate Your Inventory

Several times a year, take a hard look at the pantry to make sure items are not going to waste. When you throw away food, you are throwing away your money. Regularly check expiration dates. Pull any items that will expire in the next month and find a way to use them in a recipe.

Loss Leader

A loss leader is an item sold at or near cost that a store uses as a means to bring in patrons. Take advantage of these sales as often as possible, just be careful not to overspend on the rest of your grocery list.

Be Careful With Bulk Purchases

There is an allure to warehouse club stores, and they can, when utilized properly, cut the grocery budget significantly. While some things like toilet paper don't have an expiration date, they do take up valuable storage. Be reasonable with your purchases.

* Choosing to wear a printed muumuu on these excursions only reinforces stereotypes. And take the duck off your head.

Baking Powder Gone Bad

Dear Home-Ec 101,

The last couple times I've made drop biscuits they've been flat as a pancake. I have not altered the recipe. Can you tell me why?

Signed,
Consternated in Conyers

I am willing to bet the culprit is your baking powder. This pantry staple has a relatively short shelf life and should only be purchased in small quantities, unless you are an avid baker. Once opened, a tin of baking powder will only last three to four months in a cool, dry place. If the weather is warm and muggy, its life span will be considerably shortened. There is a simple method to test my theory. Simply add 1 teaspoon of baking powder to a half cup of hot water. If active, the baking powder will bubble in the water. If nothing happens, it's time for a new tin. When you get it, write the expiration date on the lid in permanent marker.

Some households may only need one or two items from these stores. If that's your case, consider having a friend or family member with a membership purchase the item for you and then reimburse them the cost. Don't abuse this practice. If, over time, you find yourself buying more than just the occasional jumbo pack of TP or bulk yeast for baking, it's time to pony up and get your own membership.

How Prepared Are You?

Disasters take many forms: earthquakes, hurricanes, job loss, swine flu, zombie apocalypse. Each of these would be a little easier with a cupboard full of food ready to go.

Basic emergency preparedness dictates that each household should have enough water for three days and food for two weeks, and then there are those who maintain a year's supply of food for the entire household as part of their religious practices. The amount of food a household keeps in reserve is a personal decision. Regardless of its size, a food store needs to be rotated to prevent waste. Every six months, move food from your emergency pantry to your general pantry and restock the emergency store with fresh supplies. Use up the older food in your regular meal rotation so it is not wasted. This practice ensures your emergency supply is fresh.

Make sure that the emergency portion of the pantry isn't loaded only with junk food. Items like peanut butter and canned tuna, salmon, and beans have a more useful role than empty calories like instant noodles. By all means, have some noodles on hand, but don't let those be the only provisions. It only takes a few meals of empty calories before a poor diet takes its toll.*

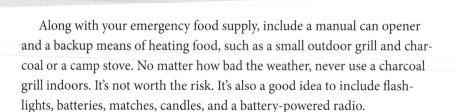

Anecdote

During a power outage, if you have the means to boil water, you can make coffee. Just pour the heated water slowly through the grounds in a filter-lined funnel. After a small hurricane knocked out power in our neighborhood, we became quite popular after the neighbors' propane ran out.

Along with your emergency food supply, include a manual can opener and a backup means of heating food, such as a small outdoor grill and charcoal or a camp stove. No matter how bad the weather, never use a charcoal grill indoors. It's not worth the risk. It's also a good idea to include flashlights, batteries, matches, candles, and a battery-powered radio.

---

* Computer code monkeys may be immune to the effects, having evolved to live on Fritos and Mountain Dew.

Pantries Save Money During Tight Times

Almost everyone has experienced being broke as a young adult. There's almost always a way to get by, which is one of the reasons Ramen has a reputation as dorm fuel. Things are a little different when there are several people living off a maxed-out paycheck. Sometimes a car repair takes priority over grocery shopping for the month. These pantry tips are not written for perfectly balanced nutrition. They are intended for short-term budget emergencies. Try to keep your protein intake as close to optimal as possible to feel healthy. If your financial situation is long term and you are in a bind, it is time to contact a food pantry or a local church for help and advice.

Inventory the Pantry, Freezer, and Refrigerator

Of course there are exceptions, but most American families have far more food than they realize on hand. It is easy to overlook foods that are not our favorite. Now is the time to pull out the lurking cans of peas or tuna, the frozen bag of mixed vegetables we intended to use but just haven't gotten around to. If food is bad, go ahead and get rid of it, but write everything down, even that last handful of chips.

Play Iron Chef

Look at your master list and create as many meals as possible. Throw out your preconceived ideas about when foods should be eaten. Spaghetti for breakfast never hurt anyone and neither has pancakes or French toast for dinner. Soups and casseroles are your friend. Now that handful of potato chips can become a topping for tuna noodle casserole.

Evil Weevils

Dear Home-Ec 101,

My food pantry is completely full of weevils. I tried fog bombs, insecticide, you name it. I took out the flour and pasta packages and put them in the fridge. I also put the rice and beans in airtight containers, but still the little buggers are there. What else needs to be done?

Signed,

Infested in Indianapolis

Meal weevils and pantry moths are the worst. You have to get rid of any flour and pasta that was open, especially anything that had a tiny hole in it—look very carefully. Take everything out of the cupboard and examine each item, throw away* anything that the moths or weevils could have gotten into, and then vacuum the living daylights out of the cupboards (including the top and bottom of the shelves, the walls, and all the corners), plus the area around and above them to get rid of larvae and eggs.

From now on, store flour, cornmeal, pasta, grits, oats, and Cream of Wheat in sealed containers. When purchasing these items, always inspect the packaging carefully. If the package is leaking, that means there is a means for entry. Don't forget to check containers of birdseed and baked dog treats, as these can also bring home infestations. I store my bulk oats in 5-gallon frosting buckets from the bakery department of our local grocery store. I only had to say please (and wash out the frosting). Before storing any grain product, place it in the freezer for forty-eight to seventy-two hours to kill any existing moths or weevils.

---

* Or don't. In a true emergency, know that the weevils and moths won't actually hurt you and even provide a little bit of protein, should you opt to ingest them.

Please don't whine that Little Johnny will only eat chicken nuggets and french fries. One of the biggest lessons life teaches us is that the world does not cater to our whims and fancies. It's better for him to receive this lesson with gentle encouragement and praise for trying new things than as an adult with potentially crushing consequences.

Gap Fillers

When planning your list, keep these ingredients in mind for stretching your limited budget as far as possible.

- *Bouillon:* Healthy? Not so much, but used wisely, these cubes can make the difference between barely edible—are we having rice *again?*—and tasty.
- *Rice* (brown if possible): Use as a side dish or use cooked rice in place of half the ground or shredded meat in a recipe with few flavor consequences. This works better if the rice is cooked with bouillon.
- *Beans/Lentils:* When served with rice, these create a complete and filling protein for a fraction of the cost of meat. Like rice, cooked beans can be added to many recipes in place of half or more of the meat. Try using lentils in place of ground beef in highly flavored dishes. Don't just think beans and rice: Think of chili, refried beans, burritos, enchiladas, etc.
- *Eggs:* Scrambled eggs, omelets, French toast, and crustless quiches are all filling and economical.
- *Rolled oats:* In addition to oatmeal, rolled oats can also be used to stretch recipes calling for ground beef or turkey in casseroles, skillets, and meat loaves. You may need to increase the liquid used in the recipe. Experiment carefully, now is not the time to waste food.
- *Potatoes:* These starchy tubers can make easy, cheap meals if necessary, or they can fill in the edges of a skimpy plate.
- *Pasta:* Think chili mac instead of just chili, spaghetti with marinara, or even buttered noodles tossed with frozen peas.

TWENTY

Meal Planning: Not Just for the Control Freaks

The 5:30 stare, we've all done it. You look into the cold, unforgiving fridge hoping something will peek out from behind the condiments and say, "Hi! I'm tasty meal and I'll be ready in just ten minutes." All too often the 5:30 stare leads to the six o'clock phone call, "I'd like to order a large . . ."

Menu plans aren't just for the uptight or the family of four. Having a plan helps a cook efficiently use her resources (time and money) to prepare healthy meals, and that benefits singles, couples, and families alike.

Form a New Dinner Habit

Couch potatoes don't turn into marathon runners overnight, and while not as strenuous a transition, it's still a big change to switch from the drive-thru to the dinner table. Nutrition gurus and frugality experts, look away for a moment. If you are new to cooking, but must put a stop to your fast-food habit, use convenience foods. Did you hear that? I just recommended dinners like Hamburger Helper or taco kits.

For the first two weeks of your menu-planning endeavor, the goal is to get used to eating at your table. Yes, that thing buried underneath the bills

Weekly Menu Idea No. 1

1. Cheeseburgers, carrot raisin salad, sweet potato wedges
2. Pulled pork barbecue over rice, broccoli, corn
3. Chicken thighs with soy and garlic, fried rice, green beans
4. Tuna noodle casserole, peas with garlic butter
5. Lemon rosemary roast chicken, roasted potatoes, steamed vegetables

and overdue library books. Your mission is to clean it off. All of it. I'll wait. If your table is the household dumping ground, you'll just have to find a new place for all that stuff—and this, my friend, can be an uphill battle, so be prepared.

Next, get a piece of paper, a writing utensil of your choice, and sit down for ten minutes. List the days of the week (no, this isn't the hard part, but a calendar could be helpful if you get stuck) and any activities that may make meal preparation difficult. In some households, it's sports activities, in others it's rotating work shifts. The point is to not plan a difficult meal for a busy night. Allow one night for leftovers. In our house we call it CORN: Clean Out Refrigerator Night. Another night is a complete break from cooking. As you gain experience with menu planning, the night off may be a meal pulled from the freezer, but for now frozen pizza or sandwiches fit the bill.

This method leaves a maximum of five dinners per week to plan. Remember, these first two weeks are only about getting used to being in the kitchen and dining room. Don't worry if the nutrition isn't perfectly balanced. This is just the first step. If you can read—and you are right now, so stop shaking your head—you can handle making spaghetti with jarred sauce. Add a couple frozen chicken patties,* and you have a cheater's

* Please cook them according to the package directions.

chicken Parmesan, just like Mom used to make. Jazz up premade salads with hard-boiled eggs, canned tuna, or grilled chicken and shrimp. Ground beef and a packet of brown gravy can be served over egg noodles or instant mashed potatoes with corn or green beans. Any of these meals can be put together in under twenty minutes and are simply a matter of following the directions on the packages.

Will these meals be served at the Four Seasons? No, but they are edible and won't break the bank as you find your kitchen legs.

Here are ten tips to successfully expand your menu.

1. Sit down with the grocery store circular to take advantage of sales when planning the week's menu.
2. If you are cooking for others, don't push your luck, only introduce one new food item per week.
3. Pay attention to the reactions of your audience. If they hate the black bean dish you tried this week, try a different main ingredient next time.
4. Be open to suggestions.
5. Different marinades make similar meals feel exotic. Grilled chicken with barbecue sauce is nothing like chicken with an Asian marinade. Additionally, using the same marinade on a variety of meats can liven up a menu. The same goes for sauces and rubs.
6. Vary your sides. Similar entrees can feel entirely different if they are served with noodles instead of mashed potatoes or sweet potatoes instead of broccoli.

Ask an Expert

Talk to people at farmers markets to find easy recipes for in-season ingredients. Many times the stand operators have a brochure with suggestions; take advantage of their experience.

Weekly Menu Idea No. 2

1. Ribs, pasta salad, roasted broccoli
2. Reubens, cream of broccoli soup, sliced apples
3. White chicken chili, cornbread
4. Spaghetti with marinara, yellow squash sautéed with garlic
5. Frittata (a crustless quiche), tossed salad

7. Learn to make soup. It's simple, economical, and there are hundreds of variations that can be created from ingredients found in the average refrigerator, freezer, and pantry. It also is a fabulous way to use leftovers.

8. If you are new to cooking, avoid fancy cooking magazines. Some are great, but others call for exotic ingredients that a beginner cook may not have on hand.* In rural areas, some of the ingredients may be difficult to find.

9. Peruse other menus. There are many online communities where people share their menu plans. They can be found by doing an online search for the term "Menu Plan."

10. Think of your favorite menu items when eating out. Set a goal to master a similar recipe. Even a beginner cook can quickly learn to outdo many middle-of-the-road chain restaurants.

Outline your plan and hang it in an obvious location. Remember that it is simply a guide to help you avoid the drive-thru. Each night before bed, glance at the menu and make sure nothing needs to be done the night before. I have kicked myself many times for forgetting to get meat from the freezer or to soak dried beans. A little forethought will help you avoid unnecessary hassle.

* Or they are overly complicated or esoteric because the magazines ran through the simple, everyday dishes years ago. Just look at some of the article titles: "Fifteen Fantastic Kale Dishes!"

Stock

This recipe can be doubled or tripled, depending on the size of your cookware and the amount of bones available.

Tools needed: large pot, colander, large bowl

Nice to have: cheesecloth, skimmer

Ingredients:

1–2 lbs various chicken bones (wing tips, backs, carcass) + contents of the giblet bag if that's available (except the liver, which looks like raw, red meat)

3 cloves of garlic

6 peppercorns

1 large carrot, scrubbed and cut into chunks

2 ribs celery, washed, cut into chunks, with the leaves

1 bay leaf

1 onion peeled, washed, and cut into quarters

6 cups of cold water

Toss all the chicken bits into your large pot then add everything else. Turn the heat to medium high and bring to a full boil. Skim off the foam that forms. Then turn the heat down to low and keep it at a simmer for at least one hour, it doesn't need any attention.

Remove the pot from the heat and pour through two layers of cheesecloth, (or a sieve, strainer, or colander) into a large bowl. Scoop out any bits. For even better stock, gather the corners of the cheesecloth and form a sack. Give it a few minutes to cool off enough to handle, then squeeze every last drop into your large bowl.

Set the stock aside for a moment and scrub out your pot. That's fun, isn't it?

Pour the stock back into the clean pot, bring to a steady simmer, and let the stock cook down until it is half of its original volume.

Don't underestimate the flavor improvement provided by substituting vegetable, chicken, or beef stock (or broth) for water when cooking vegetables or rice. If you use store-bought stock or bouillon, keep an eye on your overall sodium consumption. Use the lower sodium alternatives whenever possible.

A Healthy and Varied Menu

Once eating at home has become habit, it's time to start looking at ways to streamline the process and create a healthy and varied menu. When planning a week's menu, first plan the main dishes. Then go back and fill in the corners with appropriate side items. While fusion cuisine is all the rage in some high-end restaurants, try to center a meal on complementary flavors: chicken and rice, pork and apples, fish and chips, kibbles and bits—wait, not that last one.

Aim for two sides per meal, with at least one simple vegetable (steamed or raw) or salad. Casseroles count as both main dish and one side, and if they are packed with vegetables, they can count as all three.

Keep a rein on the number of starches you serve, whether they are of the pasta, rice, potato, or corn variety. If one of these items is used in the main dish, substitute legumes or steamed vegetables for the usual sides. For example, if rice is in the main dish, try lentil pilaf on the side instead of potatoes.

Sometimes reaching for the same vegetables several times through the course of a week is A-OK. If everyone in the house loves roasted broccoli, by all means serve it frequently.

No Effort Extras

Raw vegetables make a great addition to a soup and sandwich night. How's that for no effort?

Colorful Equals Nutritional

Add vegetables to your rice dishes. Instead of serving plain rice, try rice and peas, fried rice, or Spanish rice, which provide a lot more flavor than the plain version.

When planning meals, keep in mind that color is a big deal. As a rule of thumb, try to never serve a pale meal. If you make fettucini alfredo, serve

Weekly Menu Idea No. 3

1. Chicken, peppers and mushrooms, brussels sprouts, roast potatoes
2. Oatmeal-and-banana pancakes, scrambled eggs, fruit
3. Fish stew with a loaf of crusty bread
4. Cottage pie, green beans, spinach salad
5. Lentil casserole, spaghetti squash

it on a bed of spinach or make wilted spinach on the side. Top the dish with diced tomatoes or serve steamed baby carrots. Try to avoid the baked chicken, rice, gravy, and corn rut. Even a simple swap for steamed broccoli has a big impact. What about rice with tomato gravy for even more color? Even better. Reach for purple cabbage instead of green, if the other items aren't visually stimulating. The simple addition of black beans or bell peppers can give corn a confetti appearance. Use sweet potatoes instead of russet. As a bonus, colors are often a useful indication of nutritional content. The darker or brighter the food, the more nutrition (vitamins, antioxidants) it contains.

Don't forget there is a lot more to salad than the sad, precut iceberg salad mix in the produce section. Try different lettuces or spinach for variety.

For the biggest impact of all, try to create a flow of flavor from one item to another. This is particularly effective for big holiday-style meals that feature several items.

Avoid the Rut

I'd like to clear up this misconception right now: Habits are not ruts. The habit is what helps break the cycle of relying on the drive-thru for sustenance. In the case of menu planning, the idea of repetitively cycling through eight meals of convenience food becomes depressing, and once again the take-out option becomes appealing. To prevent the rut you must be brave and experiment. Two facts about your meal planning journey:

- As the cook it is not your job to please everyone. Take requests, but they must be reasonable. Don't cook to purposely irk your family, but don't cater to overly picky palates, either. A perk of being the planner is that your whims are the first to be accommodated after allergies and dietary restrictions.

- Accept that there are times when you will screw up or be disappointed. It's not the end of the world. It's one meal and there are very few of us in America who couldn't stand to skimp on a meal or two. Salvage the night by making popcorn or some other treat. Be careful though, some of the more inventive family members out there could figure out your plan and sabotage future efforts.

If all of this is overwhelming, try a themed approach. Assign some nights a category of meals. Mostly this is just a trick to get the creative juices flowing, no one is saying Taco Tuesday can't take place on Thursday. It's the mnemonic device that makes it easy to remember. (I'd probably skip Thankless Thursday, where you put a lot of effort into a meal and the family shrieks "I don't like it!".) I've already mentioned C.O.R.N. Here are some other ideas.

Cook in Batches

Batch cooking is both time and energy saving, as the oven runs only once or only for a short while with the second and third meal.

Meatless Monday
Eggplant parmigiana, fettuccine alfredo, quiche, rice and beans are all examples of meatless meals. They don't have to be vegetarian to fit the bill, but meat should be an accent rather than the main focus.

Meal Planning for Families

Learn to delegate. Even preschoolers can shred lettuce.* Pre-teens are perfectly capable of turning on the oven, inserting a covered dish, and setting a timer. They can also prepare salads. High schoolers should be capable of assembling an entire meal, provided the ingredients are on hand, labeled, and the instructions are clear. Empower your children by giving them the life skills they need to be self-sufficient adults.

* Don't believe me? Hand a two-year-old a roll of toilet paper. Same principle.

Taco Tuesday

Start by alternating weeks of hard and soft shells, then push the envelope and venture into shredded beef, chicken, lentil, or even fish tacos. Or forget the tacos all together and just go Tex-Mex.

Soup and Sandwich Saturday

Hearty stews, chili, and chowders are perfect in the winter, and there are a number of cold soup recipes you can serve in the summer. Or swap the soup for a salad in hot months. Get creative with your sandwich options. Use different types of breads and meats. You can even cook extra portions of meat earlier in the week and use the leftovers for your sandwiches. Try toasting or grilling the sandwiches. No need to stick to bologna and cheese.

Breakfast for Dinner a.k.a. Brinner

If your family loves breakfast foods such as pancakes, eggs, and sausage, but no one has time to eat more than a bowl of cereal in the morning, add this to the rotation. Be sure to add a side of fruit or throw some spinach in the eggs to balance the nutrition.

Pasta Night

There's so much more to pasta than plain old spaghetti. Alfredo, carbonara, primavera, Bolognese to name a few, then venture further east and try various stir-fries with mei fun or lo mein.

Stop Thinking Leftovers, Try Planned Overs

Once you get the hang of menu planning it's time to up the ante and learn the planned-over formula. The basic premise is to cook only one labor-intensive meal and roll that one item into several meals.

Take meat loaf. It's a good entree, but it's even better the next day crumbled into vegetable soup, served in sandwiches, or crumbled into spaghetti sauce. For the last variation, the spices used in the recipe must be compatible with the basil and oregano in your favorite marinara.

Singles and couples are often able to utilize the planned-over concept without resorting to doubling or tripling recipes.

Roast chicken, or as some call it, rubber chicken, is famous for its ability to transform from one meal to the next. A roast chicken on Sunday can become a chicken and rice dish on Tuesday, and chicken noodle soup or chicken potpie on Wednesday. Chicken noodle soup is a simple soup for even a beginner. Dice onions, carrots, celery, and garlic. Heat these

Confession

I once shredded the leftovers of a rosemary-seasoned pot roast and cooked them with salsa, garlic, and cumin and baked them in tortillas for oven chimichangas, (I had forgotten about the rosemary seasoning). We discovered that the rosemary clashed horribly with the other flavors and we ended up having pizza that night.

Basic Meat Loaf

1½ lbs lean ground beef
⅔ cup bread crumbs
¾ cup milk
2 eggs, beaten
¼ cup finely minced onion
1 garlic clove finely minced
1 tsp salt
fresh ground pepper

½ tsp poultry seasoning (or sage, basil, oregano, or my favorite, Cajun!*)
Optional glaze
¼ cup ketchup
1 Tbsp brown sugar
1 tsp dry mustard

*reduce the salt if using a premixed spice that contains sodium

Preheat the oven to 350° F.

Gently crumble the meat into a large bowl. The key to a tender meat loaf is to handle the meat as little as possible. To ensure easy mixing, gently separate the ground bits and make a well (depression) in the center. Sprinkle the bread crumbs (substitute crushed crackers or stuffing mix, if desired) evenly over the contents in the bowl.

In a second bowl, stir together the milk, beaten eggs, and seasoning. Mix well. Pour the wet ingredients into the well you created in the meat. With clean hands, fold the meat toward the center. Do this by grasping the side of the bowl

ingredients in a smidge of olive oil in a heavy pot over medium-low heat. When the celery turns bright green and the onions begin to look clear, add chicken stock or broth to the pot. Bring to a boil, then reduce the heat to a simmer. Season with salt, pepper, sage, thyme, and maybe a pinch of rosemary. Don't worry that there are no amounts for the seasonings. Add a pinch, stir, wait a moment and then taste. Add shredded or diced chicken, cooked noodles, heat through, and serve. Relax, you'll be fine, the soup will be great.

with one hand, to hold it steady. Slide your other hand under the meat and fold it toward the middle. Rotate the bowl and repeat. Repeat this step only until the meat is just mixed; too much handling makes a tough meat loaf. Gently pat the meat into a loaf shape on a clean baking sheet.

Bake at 350° F for approximately an hour, but check the temperature after 45 minutes and spread with the glaze, if desired. Cook for 10–15 more minutes. The meat loaf is done when it reaches 160°F in the center.

Variations:

- If using preseasoned bread crumbs, reduce the salt in the recipe.
- Try using ½ bulk Italian sausage and ½ tsp Italian seasoning.
- Some swear by a 50:50 mixture of ground pork and ground beef.
- I like to add grated vegetables such as carrot or zucchini into the mix.
- Finely diced bell pepper is a nice touch.
- When making variations that call for cheese or wet ingredients like BBQ sauce, reduce the milk.

Large beef roasts are also extremely versatile. Serve it sliced thin with roasted vegetables one day, with au jus on French bread with provolone or melted cheddar for French dips another, and shred the last little bit into soup or make a cottage pie by sweating some vegetables, adding the shredded beef, and topping with mashed potatoes and a little bit of cheese, then bake at 350° F until bubbly.

TWENTY-ONE

Substitutions: I'll Remember to Put it on the List, Promise

Every home runs out of important ingredients from time to time. Europeans blamed it on pixies.* My parents blamed it on the movers. We blame the kids. Sometimes there isn't time for a last-minute trip to the store, and sometimes it's just not worth the effort. Knowing what ingredients work as substitutes for each other is a useful skill. Once again, it's chemistry that helps explain why some substitutions are better than others.

Rising to the Occasion: Baking Soda vs. Baking Powder

Let's start simply. What's the difference between baking soda and baking powder? Baking soda is sodium bicarbonate. It's weakly alkaline and it will react with acids such as vinegar or buttermilk to create bubbles. These bubbles are what give quick breads such as muffins and cakes their loft. If baking soda does not have an acid to react with, nothing happens, and the baked good will have the bitter flavor of unreacted baking soda. Too much baking soda in a recipe can leave a salty flavor, as salts are the natural by-product of an acid-base reaction.

* Or pictsies. Crivens!

220

Baking powder is a mixture of sodium bicarbonate, cream of tartar, and a drying agent—usually a starch of some sort. The cream of tartar provides the acid for the reaction when the baking powder comes in contact with a liquid. The drawback of bringing your own acid? Baking powder can go bad, as the powder can absorb moisture from the air and react slowly. This is why baking powder comes in a covered tin and baking soda an open box.

If a recipe calls for baking soda and there is only baking powder on hand, triple the amount used, but expect a small change in flavor. If the recipe calls for baking powder, and you're out of cream of tartar, then you are out of luck. If you have cream of tartar on hand, it's two parts cream of tartar for one part baking soda. Mix thoroughly before adding to the dry ingredients.

Binding Agents

No, we're not talking about Granny and her cheese, we're talking about eggs. Eggs are the protein that holds many baked goods together. An egg starts off gelatinous, but as it is heated, the protein coagulates and sets, keeping most baked goods from being extra crumbly. There are several substitution options, and it depends on the particular recipe for which one will work the best.

** This is not to be confused with your uncle's special brownies.

Fresh or Dry Herbs

When substituting dry herbs for fresh, remember that a lot of the water has evaporated, thereby concentrating the flavor, so use one-third to one-half of the amount in the recipe.

Soy flour is fine for most baked goods, provided the eggs weren't the only liquid. If that isn't an option, flax, ground and mixed with water, works well, too. To replace one egg, grind 1 tablespoon of whole flax seeds in a clean coffee grinder and mix with 3 tablespoons of water or use 1 tablespoon of soy flour.

A Fat or Oil by Any Other Name

Fats and oils play an integral role in many recipes, and they are chosen based on several properties. Flavor, melting point, and smoke point all play an integral part in which fat is the best choice. Most vegetable oils are interchangeable: It's fine to use soybean oil and canola oil interchangeably, but don't swap a liquid vegetable oil for a solid fat. Olive oil is usually a special case, as so much of the success of the recipe depends on the quality of the oil.

Solid Fat, It's Where It's At

Butter has the lowest melting point, which causes baked goods to spread before the binding agent, such as egg or gluten, becomes firm. Margarine's melting point is only slightly higher than that of butter. Shortening's melting point is significantly higher, reducing the spread of baked goods in the oven. Commercially hydrogenated vegetable oil is extremely cheap and shelf stable. The taste is improved with extra sugar. New processes for creating shortening often use fully hydrogenated vegetable oil that does not contain trans fat. Fully hydrogenated shortening alone is too solid for cooking, so it is blended with oils such as safflower and cottonseed to produce

Smoke Points for Oils and Fats

Fat	Smoke Point
Canola Oil, High Oleic	475° F (246° C)
Canola Oil, Refined	470° F (243° C)
Corn Oil, Refined	450° F (232° C)
Corn Oil, Unrefined	320° F (160° C)
Lard	370° F (188° C)
Olive Oil, Extra Light	468° F (242° C)
Olive Oil, Extra Virgin	375° F (191° C)
Olive Oil, Pomace	460° F (238° C)
Olive Oil, Virgin	420° F (216° C)
Peanut Oil, Refined	450° F (232° C)
Safflower Oil, Refined	510° F (266° C)
Safflower Oil, Unrefined	225° F (107° C)
Soybean Oil, Refined	450° F (232° C)
Vegetable Shortening	360° F (182° C)

the proper consistency. This is being touted as a more healthful approach, but for years margarine was said to be more healthful than butter. Margarine is a term that includes a lot of different manufacturing processes, some of which contain partially hydrogenated oils. Research is changing the nutritional view of butter, margarine, and shortening. As a consumer, it's crucial to read labels.

Swapping Oils

Dear Home-Ec 101,

If a recipe calls for vegetable oil, is extra virgin olive oil a suitable replacement or is there a specific reason for vegetable oil?

Signed,

Slick in Slatesville

It depends on the recipe in question. In baking, oils are often specified for their lack of taste. So if you will be using this substitution in a baking recipe, it depends mostly on the quality of the oil you are using. If your extra virgin olive oil is the generic store brand, it is not the best oil for the job. For marinades, salad dressings, and savory sauces, extra virgin olive oil is a fantastic substitute for vegetable oil, and may even be preferable. When it comes to frying and sautéing, it depends on the manufacturer and the quality of the oil. The oil listed in fried recipes is often chosen for its smoke point. High-quality extra virgin olive oil can have a very high smoke point, above 400° F (204° C), but lesser quality versions can be significantly lower, in the 220° F (104° C) range, which is much too low to use for frying. Use your judgment when making your decision.

Lard* is simply rendered pork fat. Sounds terrible, doesn't it? When properly rendered, it is a flavorless fat that is solid at room temperature. It is a marvelous fat for certain types of baking. It does not contain water (unlike butter), which improves the texture and appearance of piecrust, especially for savory pies. It also does not contain trans fat. While lard is a useful fat, be careful if you may be serving vegetarians or those who practice kosher or halal diets. Kosher varieties can be used when necessary. Suet is rendered from cattle or sheep to make tallow.

* Anyone else remember the blueberry pie contest in *Stand by Me*? Boom baba boom.

All Flours Are Not Created Equal

Self-rising flour is also called self-raising flour. This is soft wheat flour with salt and a leavening agent (baking powder) already included. Be careful using this flour if your salt intake is restricted.

All-purpose flour is also known as plain flour. It can be found in bleached and unbleached varieties. Unbleached flour has more of the wheat's protein intact and is typically better for bread making. Bleached flour has been chemically treated to speed processing. It is best for those instances where toughness or chewiness is undesirable (piecrust, muffins, etc.). All-purpose flour is a blend of both soft and hard wheat. Different brands use different ratios of the two.

Bread flour has a higher gluten, or protein, content than all-purpose or pastry flours. The structure the protein provides makes it a good choice for baking products made with yeast. It is made from hard wheat.

Whole wheat flour, unlike white flour, uses the whole wheat kernel (surprised?). Whole wheat flour contains more fiber and is generally healthier than white flours, but it has a lower potein content. The lower protein content means there is less structure to trap air, yielding dense dough. When making breads, it is common to use a blend of whole wheat flour and bread flour or all-purpose flour to create the structure necessary to trap the carbon dioxide the yeast creates to give the bread an appealing amount of loft. Whole wheat flour can go rancid; store it in an airtight container in the fridge or freezer for the longest shelf life.

Flour Substitutions

For 1 cup Self-Rising Flour: In a 1 cup measure, place 1½ teaspoon baking powder + ½ teaspoon salt and fill the cup with plain flour.

For 2 cups of cake flour, use 1¾ cups plain or all purpose flour + ¼ cups corn starch or potato starch or tapioca starch.

For 1 cup pastry flour, use ½ cup cake flour + ½ cup all purpose flour.

Yeast Packets

When reading recipes, remember that one packet of yeast is equivalent to 2¼ teaspoons dry yeast.

Yeasty Beasties

Yeasts are tiny one-celled fungi. There are both benevolent and obnoxious strains. You can find yeast commercially for brewing, as a nutritional supplement, and for baking. In bread making, yeast digests sugars and creates carbon dioxide. The structure of the dough traps the gas, giving yeast bread its loft and softness. Too little yeast* will result in dense, heavy loaves, while too much may overwhelm the structure of the dough and cause it to either collapse on itself or create large pockets or bubbles. I am sure you have come across commercial loaves of bread with gaping holes.

There are several options when buying dry yeast:

Active dry yeast is good for longer storage but is less tolerant to thermal-shock (or a dramatic, sudden change in temperature). In other words, you need to be absolutely sure the warm water or milk used in the recipe is not hotter than 122° F (50° C). This form of yeast should also be added to a liquid before mixing into the dough, as the live cells are typically encapsulated and protected by dead cells.

Instant dry yeast is more perishable than active, but contains a higher percentage of live cells. It may be added directly to the dough. However, a small amount should always be tested to ensure it is viable.

Rapid rise yeast is a form of instant yeast developed to reduce rising time. It is believed to produce a less flavorful product, but it is useful in some bread machine recipes.

In my experience, our local grocery store carries yeast only in the tiny packets or jars. Neither option is particularly budget conscious. Warehouse

---

*   While no yeast and a healthy handful of gravel yields dwarven bread.

club stores or some restaurant supply stores will sell yeast in two-pound packages for approximately the cost of three small packets. Dry yeast should last at least six months in the freezer. If you divide it before storage, it may last over a year, but that shelf life is not guaranteed. It is always important to test the yeast to be sure it is still viable. If you are just starting out on your bread-baking journey, don't make bulk yeast your very first purchase. Wait until you've had several successes before committing to the large bag, as no one needs a constant reminder of a failed project each time they open the freezer. Allow frozen yeast to come to room temperature before using.

The other option when purchasing yeast is to buy it fresh. It may be found packaged in cakes (like cakes of soap) and is sold under the names fresh yeast, cake yeast, baker's compressed yeast, or wet yeast. This is often stocked at health food or restaurant supply stores and is highly perishable.

When substituting in recipes calling for dry yeast, remember one small cake of fresh or compressed yeast is 0.6 oz and is equivalent to 2¼ teaspoons dry yeast. To test yeast for viability, add a pinch to a weak solution of warm sugar water. The yeast should make tiny bubbles that produce a creamy foam. Finally, remember that nutritional (or brewer's) yeast is not the same as yeast for baking or brewing. It is dead—like Elvis—and will not produce the gas necessary for rising.

Sweet Like Candy

Be careful substituting one sugar for another. Brown sugar** can easily be replaced with 1 cup white sugar and 2 tablespoons molasses, but you'll need to mix it thoroughly before you add it to the recipe. Sugar substitutes won't always act just like sugar in a recipe, but Splenda is close. Honey can be used in place of sugar, but in baked goods other liquids in the recipe may need to be reduced. Never experiment with a sugar substitute if you are cooking for company or an event such as a bake sale. Always practice

** How come you look so good?

to see how the results affect the recipe. Understand that some sugar substitutes still affect the blood sugar of diabetics; using these items is not a license to gorge.

Dairy

Dairy is a complicated beast, with udders, lots of udders. Sometimes dairy's role is purely liquid. In these cases, it doesn't matter whether it's skim, two percent, or whole milk. Other times, though, the milk provides much needed fat content, which strongly affects how rich a recipe tastes. Tread carefully when reducing the fat content by switching from heavy cream to half-and-half to whole milk. Each step down is a significant change, and there will be taste consequences. In savory dishes, consider replacing some of the dairy with the appropriate chicken, fish, or vegetable stock.

Plain yogurt and sour cream are interchangeable to a point. As long as other flavors are incorporated, it's fairly easy to switch between the two with little consequence. But most people wouldn't want plain yogurt on their tacos or sour cream in their health shake.

Substitutions Aren't Always An Emergency

Sometimes switching ingredients can create a pleasing variation on a recipe. Switch dried cranberries for raisins; try pecans in place of walnuts. Use almond extract in place of vanilla. However, it's important when venturing down this path to understand the role of the ingredient being

Add Flavor, Not Sodium

Strong flavors help reduce a dependence on salt as a flavoring. Try increasing your other favorite flavors and reducing the amount of salt used in recipes.

Rules to Remember When Substituting Meats

1. Shape matters more than weight. Long, thin cuts will cook faster than short, thick ones of the same weight. The more surface area exposed to heat, the faster a cut of meat will cook and dry out.
2. A boneless cut of meat cooks more slowly than a bone-in cut of the same size.
3. A fat cap (that is fat that surrounds a cut of meat) acts as an insulator and can increase the cooking time.

changed. Sometimes liquids play an important acidic role in the recipe; this is especially true for marinades and the liquid used in a recipe for braising. Vinegars can generally be swapped for other flavored vinegars without adjustment, but there will be a flavor difference. Lemon juice is a good substitute for vinegar, but white wine may not be acidic enough in place of vinegar. Infused olive oils are also a great way to shake up a recipe; try garlic- or rosemary-infused olive oil in a marinade, but avoid these for sautéing, as they can burn more easily.

Swapping Cuts of Meat

All cuts of meat are not equal. In poultry, chicken has both white and dark meat.* Remember that pound for pound, white meat cooks faster than dark meat, and there is less connective tissue in white meat. A recipe intended for boneless, skinless chicken breasts may need a little more cooking time if boneless thighs are substituted.

Make friends with the butcher, even at the grocery store. Part of his job is to explain the cuts of meat. The names of cuts aren't always a useful

---

* If there are other colors present, throw out the chicken.

Emergency Cooking or Baking Substitutions

Ingredient	Amount	Substitutions
Baking Powder	1 TBSP	2 tsp cream of tartar and 1 tsp baking soda (measure needed amount from this mixture)
Baking Soda	1 tsp	3 tsp baking powder
Buttermilk	1 cup	1 TBSP white vinegar or lemon juice + enough milk to equal 1 cup. Let stand 5 minutes, stir.
Cornstarch	1 TBSP	2 TBSP all-purpose flour or 1 TBSP potato or tapioca starch
Egg	1	2½ TBSP ground flaxseed or 1 TBSP whole flaxseed, ground + 3 TBSP water, beaten (for use in baked goods); or 1 TBSP soy flour; or 2 egg whites; or 2 egg yolks; (each of these has their own unique properties)

indication of where the meat came from. A perfect example is a Boston butt. It's a cut of pork that is great for making pulled pork and hash, and no, it doesn't come from the butt of a pig. The cut is actually from the shoulder, and the name originates from the barrels (once called butts) the cuts used to be stored in. When selecting cuts of meat, a good rule of thumb is the more the muscle was used, the tougher the meat will be. Active muscles will also have more connective tissue. Muscular cuts of meat need a slow, wet cooking method. Save the grilling, sautéing, and broiling for the less exercised, more tender cuts of meat.

Ingredient	Amount	Substitutions
Ginger Root, Fresh	1 tsp grated	¾ to 1 tsp dried
Honey	1 cup	1¼ cup white sugar + ¼ cup apple juice or watermelon
Hot Pepper Sauce	a few drops	⅛ tsp cayenne pepper
Ketchup	1 cup	1 cup tomato sauce, ½ cup sugar, 2 TBSP vinegar (for cooking, not dipping)
Lemon Juice	1 TBSP	1 TBSP white vinegar (for acidic purposes, not flavor)
Yeast	1 package	2¼ tsp regular or quick active; or 1 package compressed yeast cake
Plain Yogurt	1 cup	1 cup sour cream

Homemade Cleaning Solutions

Before using any cleaner, check with the manufacturer of the object you are cleaning to ensure it is in line with their recommendations. Use common sense and always test in an inconspicuous area.

General Cleaning Spray

1:1 white vinegar and water

Do not use this acidic cleaner on marble.

General Cleaning Spray II

2 tsp borax

4 TBSP white vinegar

½ tsp dish soap

3 cups hot water

Spray on, sponge off.

Toilet Bowl Cleaner

Straight white vinegar

Allow to soak overnight, then scrub in the morning.

Vinyl Floors

Mix 1 gallon water

½ cup white vinegar or ¼ cup borax

Remove scuff marks with toothpaste.

Mold Removal

1 part hydrogen peroxide (3%)*

2 parts water

Spray and allow to sit for 1 hour before wiping. Or use isopropyl (rubbing) alcohol, provided it is safe for use on the intended surface. Avoid inhaling the fumes.

*Hydrogen peroxide breaks down quickly, so mix it fresh each time.

Dusting Solution

Use a soft, damp cloth. Microfiber is an excellent choice.

Window Cleaner

1 quart warm water

¼ cup white vinegar or 2 TBSP lemon juice

Mix ingredients and store in a spray bottle.

Dangerous Chemical Combinations

If switching from one cleaning agent to another, it's important to rinse the surface carefully to remove all traces of the first product.

Wear gloves when handling chemicals. Some can cause chemical burns or irritation. Always clean in a well-ventilated area and bring in a fan if necessary.

 ### Do Not Mix These Chemicals

Chemical 1	Chemical 2	Reason
Bleach	*Ammonia*	Depending on the amount mixed, either chlorine gas (deadly) or nitrogen trichloride, a volatile explosive, is created. Hydrazine is also produced in a very exothermic (heat-producing) reaction.
Bleach	*Vinegar*	This is an acid-base reaction that produces chlorine gas. Never use a frugal home-cleaning solution that mixes these ingredients. I have seen recipes containing this dangerous combo on many homemaking websites and forums.
Bleach	*Toilet Bowl Cleaner*	Some toilet bowl cleaners are strongly acidic and can react violently, producing chlorine gas.
Toilet Bowl Cleaner Brand X	*Toilet Bowl Cleaner Brand Y*	Never mix brands, they may be acidic or alkaline in nature and could react strongly.

Emergency Preparedness Checklist

This will get most households through most minor emergencies. An online search for the term "Bug Out Bag" will provide a wealth of information on more thorough emergency preparedness.

- Minimum of three gallons of water per household member. Replace this supply every six months.
- Nonperishable food, for a minimum of three days
    peanut butter
    canned soups
    beans
    canned tuna, chicken, salmon
    canned vegetables
    crackers
    powdered milk/evaporated milk
- Manual can opener
- Camp stove or outdoor grill and fuel
- Waterproof matches
- First aid kit
- Two-week supply of prescriptions
- Battery- or crank-powered radio and flashlight
- Extra batteries
- Cash
- Extra set of car and house keys
- Sanitary supplies for women
- Change of clothes and sturdy shoes for each household member
- Blankets or sleeping bags
- Moist towelettes, garbage bags and plastic ties for personal sanitation
- Wrench or pliers to turn off utilities

Measurements Conversion Charts

Liquid Measures

1 cup	8 fluid ounces	½ pint	237 ml
2 cups	16 fluid ounces	1 pint	474 ml
4 cups	32 fluid ounces	1 quart	946 ml
2 pints	32 fluid ounces	1 quart	0.964 liters
4 quarts	128 fluid ounces	1 gallon	3.784 liters
1 gallon	128 fluid ounces	16 cups	4 quarts
8 quarts	one peck	32 cups	16 pints
4 pecks	one bushel	128 cups	64 pints

Dry Measures

3 teaspoons	1 tablespoon	½ ounce	14.3 grams	0.03 pounds
2 tablespoons	⅛ cup	1 ounce	28.3 grams	6 teaspoons
4 tablespoons	¼ cup	2 ounces	56.7 grams	12 teaspoons
5⅓ tablespoons	⅓ cup	2.6 ounces	75.6 grams	15.9 teaspoons
8 tablespoons	½ cup	4 ounces	113.4 grams	1 stick butter
12 tablespoons	¾ cup	6 ounces	.375 pound	170 grams
32 tablespoons	2 cups	16 ounces	1 pound	453.6 grams
64 tablespoons	4 cups	32 ounces	2 pounds	907 grams

Index

acetone, 94–95, 128
acidic solutions, 16–18
alcohol
    denatured, 85
    isopropyl (rubbing), 17,
        46, 51, 55–56, 60–61,
        63–64, 99
alkaline solutions, 16–18
allergies, 19, 29, 86, 215
ammonia, 15, 17, 23, 36,
    94–95, 97
appliances, 133. *See also*
    clothes dryers; dishwash-
    ers; freezers; garbage
    disposals; hot water heat-
    ers; HVAC units; micro-
    wave ovens; refrigerators;
    vacuum cleaners; washing
    machines
    cleaning, 28, 48–49
    distressed, 129
    gas, 133–134
    maintaining, 23
    repairing, 132–141
    small, 180–181
    stainless steel, 49–50

baking powder, 203, 220–221
baking soda, 44, 59, 104,
    220–221
Bar Keepers Friend, 18, 42, 44,
    51, 173–174
bathrooms, 58–63
    cleaning, 24–25, 27–28,
        54–67
    unclogging sinks in, 149

ventilation in, 56
    wiping down, 24–25
bathtubs
    acrylic, 57–58
    cleaning, 57, 59
    cleaning clogs in,
        150–151
    cleaning jets in, 62
    waxing, 61
bedding, 24–25, 83–84,
    86–88
bedrooms, cleaning, 80–88
beef roast, 219
beeswax, 52
blankets, 30–31, 43
bleach
    chlorine, 15, 19, 35, 51,
        56, 60, 62, 65, 91, 94, 96,
        100, 117, 145, 233
    nonchlorine, 117
    oxygen, 96, 98
blinds, 29, 70–71
borax, 57, 98, 103–104
brooms, 19, 33, 43
buckets, 20, 43
buttons, replacing 109

cabinets, cleaning, 28, 45–46,
    48
carbon monoxide detectors,
    129
carnauba wax, 61
carpeting
    burns in, 158–159
    care of, 37–39
    repairs to, 157–160

spot-treating, 40–41
stains on, 39–41, 158–159
steam cleaning, 40
types of, 38
vacuuming, 25, 40
caulk, 30, 63
ceiling fans, 69–70, 84
chemicals, combining, 15, 233
chicken, roast, 217
chicken noodle soup,
    217–218
children, 13, 27, 166
chimneys, cleaning, 31
circuit breakers, 131–132
citric acid, 57
cleaners. *See also* detergents;
    disinfectants
    abrasive, 18, 36, 57
    acidic, 57
    bathroom, 18
    degreasers, 17–18, 43, 45,
        49, 51, 56
    enzymatic, 39, 93, 105
    floor, 18, 35, 232
        glass, 17–18, 57, 64–65,
            72, 74
    homemade, 232
    multisurface, 17
    oil-based, 36
    stainless steel, 50
    toilet bowl, 18, 57,
        232–233
    window, 17, 232
clogs
    in bathtubs and showers,
        150–151

in sinks, 148–149
in toilets, 144–145
closets, cleaning, 80–82
clothes dryers, 119, 138–139.
   See also laundry
clothes hangers, 80–81
clothes washers. See washing
   machines
clothing
   repair of, 106–111
   storing, 122
clutter, clearing, 54–55, 68,
   82–83
cobwebs, 30, 55–56, 69, 84
cookbooks, selection of,
   163–164
cooking, 7–8, 162–169
   basic techniques, 182–197
   terminology, 186–192
cookware, 163, 170–180. See
   also pots and pans
   stainless steel, 173
cornstarch, 99
corners, cleaning, 55–56, 84
countertops, 28, 51
cream of tartar, 104
cutting boards, 51, 178

dental floss, cleaning with, 42,
   44, 64
detergents, 16, 49, 94–95, 97.
   See also cleaners
   dish, 36–37, 42, 53
   dishwasher, 60, 62
   laundry, 59, 101, 113,
      116–117
dining rooms, cleaning, 68–79
dishes, 179
   washing, 24, 44
dishwashers, 44, 137–138

disinfectants, 19, 45. See also
   cleaners
doormats, 31–33
doors, 28, 31, 73, 131
downspouts, 31, 127
drains
   clogged, 67, 144–151
   drain cleaners, chemical,
      148
   removing items from, 150
drawstrings, 107
drawers, cleaning, 46–48
dust mites, 19, 84, 86
dusting, 17–18, 23, 28–29, 69,
   73, 83–84
   electronics, 73–75
dustpans, 19, 43

eggs, 185, 207, 221
electric cords, untangling,
   74–75
electrical hazards, 124–126
emergency preparedness,
   203–205, 234
entertaining, 194–197
entryways, 25, 31–33
environmental considerations,
   15–16, 23
equipment. See also tools
   for cleaning, 19–21
   for kitchens, 171, 177–181
   for plumbing, 143

fabrics
   fabric markers, 122
   protecting, 91
   stains on, 90–99
   washing instructions for,
      114–115
fats, 222–224

faucets
   cleaning aerators on, 44
   water spots on, 65
feather dusters, 69, 78
filters, 19, 29, 134
fire extinguishers, 130
fires, dealing with, 131
floors, 25, 56
   cleaning, 27, 32–41
   repairing, 157–160
   types of, 13, 36–37
foundations, repairing, 127
foxtail brushes, 43, 51
freezers, and power failures,
   205
furniture
   cleaning, 25, 27, 75–76
   felt pads on, 37
   maintaining, 23
   repairing, 128
   types of, 13
   upholstered, 78–79
   used, 129
furniture polish, 17–18, 36,
   75–76
fuse boxes, 131–132

garbage disposals, 136–137
gaskets, 135
glassware, 179
grease. See also odors, from
   grease; stains, grease
   and drains, 148
   removing, 17
grout, 20, 37, 60–61
gutters, 30–31, 127

hair, 149–159
hedges, trimming, 131
hemlines, 108–109

holiday menus, 194, 196–197
home maintenance and repair, 7, 124–131
hoses, 31
hot water heaters, 31, 134–135
HVAC units, 13, 134
    inspecting, 29–31
hydrogen peroxide, 60

ingredients, for recipes, 185, 220–231
ink, and solvent, 91
in-line shutoff valves, 148

kitchens
    cleaning, 24–25, 28, 42–53
    cross-contamination in, 168
    equipment for, 171
    unclogging sinks in, 148–149
knives, 175–176, 189–192

Laundromats, 119–121
laundry, 6, 24–25, 112–122.
    See also clothes dryers; washing machines
        hampers, 13, 24, 54
        wet, 102
lead, testing for, 153
leaks, 30, 131
left to right, cleaning from, 45, 51
leftovers, 24, 217
lemon juice, 52, 98
light bulbs, 55, 131
light fixtures, cleaning, 29, 43, 55, 69
lighting, outdoor, 131
limescale, 58

liner mats, 46
living rooms, cleaning, 68–79
loss leaders, 202

meal planning, 194–197, 208–219
meals, premade, 196–197
measurement conversion, 235
meat loaf, 217–219
menu ideas, weekly, 209, 211, 214
microfiber cloth, 73–74
microwave ovens, 45, 167, 180
mildew, 85, 98, 100, 102–103
mineral oil, 51–52
mirrors, cleaning, 63–64, 72, 84
mold, 85, 232
monosodium glutamate (MSG), 183
mopping, 25, 27, 51, 67
mops, 20, 34–35

natural gas, 131, 133–134
nutrition, 213–214

odors, 100–105
    in bathrooms, 67
    body odor, 102–104
    chemical, 104
    in garbage disposals, 136
    from grease, 105
    from potatoes, 66
    urine, 105
oils, 222–224
    smoke points of, 223
organization, 10–11, 21
oxalic acid, 173–174

paint, 153–154

paint remover, 95
pantries, 205
    cleaning, 31
    stocking, 198–207
pantry moths, 206
patio furniture, 30–31
pictures
    cleaning, 72, 84
    hanging, 155–157
plants, fake, 76, 78
plumbing, 126, 142–151
plungers, 143, 149
pots and pans, 28, 171–176.
    See also cookware
    scorched, 174
    seasoning, 176
power, cooking without, 204

quantity, cooking in, 215

recipes, 210
    following, 184–189
    halving and doubling, 192–193
refrigerators
    cleaning, 28, 48
    troubleshooting, 135–136
    vacuuming coils, 48–49, 135
repairs, garment, 106–111
    buttonholes, 110
    zippers, 107–108
    hire out, 111

safety issues, 129–131
    and cooking, 168–169
salt, 44, 98, 182
saponification, 16
screens, inspecting, 30
scuff marks, removing, 48

sewage backups, 151
sewage lines, 67
shades, 70–71
sheers, 70–71
shoes, 12–13, 25, 82–83
showers
cleaning, 24, 57
clogs in, 150–151
glass doors in, 63
shower curtains, 57–58, 65
showerheads, 57
stains in, 65
steam from, 13
shutters, cleaning, 71
sinks
cleaning, 43–44
unclogging, 148–149
smoke alarms, 30–31, 129
snow removal, 127
soap, 16–18
soap scum, 58, 61
soups, making, 211
squeegees, 20, 24, 60, 63
stains, 90–99, 117
on carpet, 40–41, 158–159
dye, 97, 99
on fabrics, 90–99
grease, 93, 99
makeup, 99
oil, 93
potty-training, 96
protein, 92–93
rust, 60
stain treatment chart, 94–95
sweat, 102–104
tannin, 93, 97

staples, for pantries, 200–201
bulk purchase of, 202–203
steel wool, 36
stock, recipe for, 212
substitutions, cooking or baking, 220–231
surfactants, 17–18
sweeping, 25, 33–34, 51, 67
switch plates, 28, 73

talcum powder, 99
tea tree oil, 19
television screens, 73–74
termites, 127
throw rugs, 27, 33
toilets
cleaning, 20–21, 56–57, 66–67
fixing, 142–148
low-flow, 144
running, 146–147
unclogging, 144–145
tools. See also equipment
basic, 125
for carpet repair, 157–160
for cooking, 186
for wall repair, 152–154
tree roots, in pipes, 147
tri-sodium phosphate, 155
turpentine, 95

urine, 77, 79, 105
utensils, 173, 179

vacuum cleaners, 19, 139–141
with crevice tool, 25

with soft bristle attachment, 28, 43
vacuuming, 24–25, 28, 33
vanities, cleaning, 63–64
vectors, 96
vinegar, white, 19, 43, 45, 54–55, 57, 59, 62–64, 66, 73, 91, 94–95, 97, 101–102, 233

wallpaper, removing, 154–155
walls, 13, 29–30, 72
fixing, 152–157
washing machines, 112, 139.
See also laundry
cleaning, 100–101
high efficiency, 96, 102
odors in, 100–101
water damage, 126–127
water heaters. See hot water heaters
water
hardness of, 17
storing, 234
wax, on bathtubs, 61
wax ring, of toilet, 147–148
weevils, in pantry, 206
wicking, 91–92
window treatments, 70–71
windows, 31, 131
cleaning, 30–31, 71–72
wiring, problems with, 124–126
wood, polishing, 53

yard maintenance, 29

zippers, 107–108

Books of Interest

I Garden: Urban Style

Grow delicious vegetables and beautiful flowers in your urban setting. No yard? No problem. No time? No worries. *I Garden: Urban Style* is full of countless options for growing gardens that fit the smallest spaces and tightest schedules. ISBN-13: 978-1-4403-0556-6; ISBN-10: 1-4403-0556-0, paperback, 160 pages, #Z7445

Living Large on Less

You don't have to be a financial whiz (or even mathematically inclined) to manage your money. *Living Large on Less* is full of hundreds of ways to save money without drastically altering your lifestyle. You can eat the food you want, wear your favorite designer's clothes, and take a dream vacation without breaking the bank. With this advice, you'll never pay full-price again. ISBN-13: 978-1-4403-0432-3; ISBN-10: 1-4403-0432-7, paperback, 224 pages, #Z7133

Organized Simplicity

Simplicity isn't about what you give up. It's about what you gain. When you remove the things that don't matter, you are free to focus on only the meaningful. Imagine your home and your time filling you with positive energy to help you achieve your dreams. It can happen, and *Organized Simplicity* can show you how. ISBN-13: 978-1-4403-0263-3; ISBN-10: 1-4403-0263-4, hardcover with concealed spiral, 256 pages, #Z6515

These books and other fine Betterway Home titles are available at your local bookstore and from online suppliers. Visit our website at www.betterwaybooks.com.